MW00648454

HALF MY WORLD

FRONTISPIECE *An unpublished poem by Anne Spencer written on a page of Dreer's Garden Book of 1931.*

REBECCA T. FRISCHKORN & REUBEN M. RAINEY

HALF MY WORLD

The Garden of Anne Spencer
A History and Guide

Warwick House Publishing
720 Court Street
Lynchburg, Virginia 24504

ISBN 1-890306-51-7
Library of Congress Card Number: 2003111208

FRONTISPIECE
The text of Anne Spencer's unpublished poem on a page of Dreer's Garden Book of 1931 reads:

Not many things I know nor do,
But one:
This my poor heart
So vacant and so frank
Can love you
Can love you
and dispossess
itself of content
and of strength.

Printed in the United States
Book Design by Suzanne Dvells Morrish

DEDICATION

Dedicated with admiration and gratitude to
ANNE AND CHAUNCEY SPENCER
for their generous assistance and friendship.

ACKNOWLEDGMENTS

We are grateful to many people for their help in the research and preparation of the manuscript.

Chauncey Spencer shared with us his wealth of first-hand knowledge of his mother and her garden. Anne Howard Spencer, the daughter-in-law of the poet Anne Spencer, expanded upon Chauncey's stories with her own personal recollections and answered many questions, especially about daily life at 1313 Pierce Street. Carol Spencer Read, granddaughter of Anne Spencer, helped locate numerous family photographs, as well as garden magazines and nursery catalogs in the poet's collection and made valuable editorial suggestions. Kyle Spencer Thompson, also a granddaughter of the poet, offered an insightful critique of our work. Jane Baber White generously shared archival materials in the collection of the Southern Memorial Association, as well as her personal knowledge and research on the history of the garden. She also provided valuable information about the restoration of the garden, which was so skillfully and professionally carried out under her supervision. Ted Delaney, Curator and Archivist of the Old City Cemetery in Lynchburg, Virginia, was helpful in the identification of photographs in the Southern Memorial Association archives. The Anne Spencer House and Garden Museum, Inc., under the leadership of Hugh Jones, offered ongoing encouragement and support. Board members Nina Salmon and Lynch Christian provided access to valuable archival materials as well as personal reminiscences. Sandra Wilson shared her photographs of the garden as well as her time and expertise in grant preparation. Former board member Carl Hester, Mary Frances

Williams Professor of Religion at Randolph-Macon Woman's College, called our attention to several important articles on the garden. Melanie Christian provided valuable networking support as well as delicious meals to sustain our spirits. At the Lynchburg Museum System, Jill Landen, Curator of Collections, and Rachel Deddens, Assistant Curator of Collections, substantially aided our research. K. Ian Grandison, University Professor of American Studies and Landscape Architecture at the University of Virginia, and Marlon B. Ross, Professor of English and African-American Studies at the University of Virginia, read the manuscript in its entirety and made numerous helpful suggestions based on their extensive knowledge of African-American literature and cultural history. Barbara Rockefeller, former Professor of American History at Middlebury College, called our attention to several valuable sources on the history of the Harlem Renaissance. Emmanuel Didier created an exquisitely rendered watercolor plan of the garden. The Virginia Foundation for the Humanities gave its generous support for the project through a grant to the Anne Spencer House and Garden Museum, Inc. from the African-American Heritage Program. Sue Rainey gave us the gift of her professional editing skills as well as countless hours of typing the manuscript and ongoing moral support and encouragement. Carl Frischkorn offered valuable suggestions for the improvement of the manuscript, and his support of the project from the earliest stages was invaluable. Finally, Suzanne Dvells Morrish provided her highly professional skills as a graphic designer to create a beautiful example of the art of the book.

REBECCA T. FRISCHKORN & REUBEN M. RAINEY
Charlottesville, Virginia

CONTENTS

THE CREATORS OF THE GARDEN
ANNE AND EDWARD SPENCER

GARDEN SANCTUARIES CULTIVATE POETRY. The voices of poets have resonated in the Medici villas of Renaissance Italy, the Imperial villas of seventeenth-century Japan, the Persian tomb gardens of Islamic saints, the castle gardens of medieval France, and many others. A garden provides the solitude and tranquility that nurture creativity. It can serve the poet in other ways. Often the engaging presence of the garden itself, its processes of growth, decay, and transformation, its sounds, textures, tastes, fragrances, and visual delights, touch the deepest levels of the human spirit and quicken the poetic imagination. The language of the poet is infused with the alchemy of the garden. The garden both shelters and cultivates the poet.

One such garden was created by Anne Spencer, a distinguished poet of the Harlem Renaissance, in collaboration with her husband, Edward. The protagonist in Anne Spencer's poem, "Any Wife to Any Husband," muses, "This small garden is half my world..." One could say the same about Spencer's own garden. It was her private world, the place where she penned her poems in solitude and immersed herself in the reverie of gardening [fig. 1]. It was also a social realm, a gathering place for family and friends [fig. 2]. Outside her garden wall, the other half of Spencer's world involved active engagement as a librarian and educator in the segregated public school system of Lynchburg, Virginia, and as a civil rights advocate and co-founder of the local chapter of the National Association for the Advancement of Colored People (NAACP). She also was responsible for the nurturing and education of her three children and the care of her elderly mother.

This book is about Anne Spencer's garden world, its creation, development, and restoration, and, most of all, its place in her life as a poet. It is both a history and a guide.

Anne Spencer was born in Henry County, Virginia, on February 6,

1882. The only child of divorced parents, Annie Bethel Scales was the much-cherished daughter of a devoted mother who moved her to Bramwell, West Virginia, and placed Annie in the care of a leading family of the African-American community there while she worked full time as a cook. Annie was given many freedoms and privileges, including access to a rich, albeit random, collection of books. She developed a deep bond with the world of nature at the early age of six. Recalling a year spent with a family in Winston-Salem, North Carolina, before her move to Bramwell, she remarked:

> That year was good for me. It poled (sic) a feeling for the actual earth itself that I had inborn, suffused and enlightened, without which nothing that one is born in has lift or meaning, but somehow and somewhere one must make contact, touch earth, and be willing to share earth...[1]

During this same year her early ventures in landscape design were "patted up" sand piles, which she christened "ant hotels." During her childhood in Bramwell she continued her encounters with the natural world with enthusiasm, venturing to the reservoir to catch frogs or observing snakes in the river with her best friend, Elsie Brown. Often she sought solitude in woods and fields near her home, collecting wildflowers, listening to the calls of birds, or just sitting on the riverbank alone with her memories and dreams. At the age of eleven Annie was enrolled in the Virginia Seminary[2] in Lynchburg, Virginia, where she might engage in a more orderly and focused pursuit of a good education. The Seminary contained a "college" which focused on the humanities and sciences and was separate from the degree program for students planning to enter the ministry. She excelled in courses in the humanities, especially history and English literature. She also studied three years of Latin, one of French, and one of German. She was a keen student of psychology and a spirited debater. As a student of the college, she often participated in lively discussions with the theology students at the Seminary. By the age of fourteen she had written her first poem, entitled "The Skeptic," now lost, dealing with theological issues, and had begun to develop her habit of expressing her private reflections in poetry. While strong in the humanities, she was weak in science and math, and a fellow student, Edward Alexander Spencer, volunteered to tutor her in those subjects. She helped him with languages. In 1899 Annie graduated and delivered the valedictorian's address to her class. Shortly after graduation, she was given a four-volume set of the writings of Ralph Waldo Emerson. She immersed herself in Emerson's philosophy, and it became a major influence on her life and work as a poet. While her formal education had lasted only six years, she had developed a keen analytical mind and commitment to intellectual inquiry, which she pursued throughout her life.

Two years after graduation, Annie Spencer married her tutor, Edward Alexander Spencer, on May 15, 1901 [figs. 3, 4]. They established their residence in Lynchburg that same year, and within two years moved to 1313 Pierce Street into a Queen Anne-style house[3] Edward had designed on the site of Camp Davis, a former Confederate Army recruitment camp. By 1906, Annie had given birth to two daughters, Bethel Calloway and Alroy Sarah, and a son, Chauncey Edward. Here she began work on her garden.

Lynchburg in 1900 was an economically prosperous town of about nineteen thousand inhabitants. It had been established in 1786 by Quakers, most of whom had moved to the Midwest by the time of the Civil War, since they were unable to reconcile the emerging Virginia economy based on slavery with their own religious convictions. From the beginning of the nineteenth century until the Civil War, a flourishing free black community had emerged, which ranged from 12 to 26 percent of the African-American population.[4] Many of Lynchburg's early twentieth-century citizens who negotiated its steep streets and hills overlooking the James River prospered from its New South manufacturing economy marked by the smoke spewing from its cotton mills, foundries, and shoe factories. The pungent aroma of tobacco-processing plants wafted through the streets in certain sections, although tobacco was no longer the fulcrum of Lynchburg's prosperity. Its per capita income was one of the highest in the nation and its population was to swell to about forty thousand by 1930.[5]

In the midst of a highly stratified and segregated culture supported by stringent Jim Crow laws of the late nineteenth century was a vibrant African-American community comprising in 1900 about 44 percent of the population. During and after Reconstruction, African-Americans had established an extensive independent network of civic organizations, law firms, medical practices, and self-owned businesses. Social life tended to center in their churches, such as Court Street Baptist, Trinity United Methodist, and Eighth Street Baptist, the home church of Annie and Edward.[6] Annie's alma mater, Virginia Seminary, supported by the Virginia Baptist State Convention, with its broad curriculum of classics, languages, science, and theological studies, attracted African-American students from out of state. The Spencers' new home was in the western portion of the "College Hill" area of town, where Edward contributed to the quality of the community with his well-planned housing developments. Many African-American professionals and business owners settled in the area. A later neighbor of the Spencers was Dr. Walter Johnson, a local medical practitioner who was also a gifted athlete and tennis coach. His concrete tennis court adjacent to his house was the early training ground for community children and champions such as Althea Gibson and Arthur Ashe.

The natural setting of Lynchburg was a gift to gardeners. Situated in the foothills of the Blue Ridge Mountains, its temperate climate and fertile soil invited a wide-ranging plant palette. Spring and autumn were its most attractive seasons, and its residential garden art typically featured spring bloom and autumn color: dogwoods, redbuds, maples, tulip poplars, cherry trees, oaks, walnuts, mountain laurel, boxwood, azaleas, rhododendrons, sumac, roses, crocus, daffodils, tulips, bluebells, chrysanthemums, and various wildflowers from mountain meadows. In the days before air conditioning, gardens were highly cherished outdoor rooms, offering much-needed respite from the humid inferno of late summer when temperatures averaged in the 90s. Regarding Virginia gardens, Thomas Jefferson had noted, "Shade is our Elysium." In early twentieth-century Virginia gardens pergolas, arbors, and mature deciduous trees provided shade for a rich and diverse social life of garden parties, family play, and informal visits. Cool summer nights in the garden were supported by night lighting, and the abundant population of migratory and local birds helped to control the insects. Winters that could witness as much as three feet of snow prohibited year-round use of these outdoor rooms, except on occasional balmy January and February days.

Annie Spencer's life in Lynchburg was multifaceted: Although she enjoyed the creative outlets of domesticity and child rearing, she delegated many of those duties to housekeepers so she could focus her energies on her poetry and her garden, as well as her involvement in civil rights issues. Spencer participated in the founding of the local chapter of the NAACP in 1918. Through this activity she met the noted African-American diplomat, poet, composer, publisher, and writer, James Weldon Johnson [fig. 5], who, as Field Secretary of the NAACP, was traveling throughout the country to assist in the formation of local chapters. Johnson encouraged her commitment to poetry—hitherto private and personal—and with his support and direction she published her first poem, "Before the Feast of Shushan,"[7] in 1920 in *The Crisis*, the national publication of the NAACP. When Johnson edited his *Book of American Negro Poetry* in 1922, he included five of Anne Spencer's poems and officially recognized her as a member of the Harlem Renaissance, a movement embracing the artistic and literary activity of African-Americans throughout the country from about 1910 to 1930 and identified with Harlem, its symbolic center. Her poem "Lady, Lady" was published in 1925 by Alain Locke in his influential anthology, *The New Negro*.[8] Following this, she published additional poems in a number of periodicals and was Virginia's only African-American and the only woman from the state to be published in the first edition of *The Norton Anthology of Modern Poetry*.[9] James Weldon Johnson suggested her pen name "Anne Spencer," and she adopted it. (She could have used "Annie," her given name.)

While Anne Spencer was deeply involved with her poetry and the design of her garden, her life included many other interests and activities. From 1912 to 1914, she taught at her alma mater, which had become the "Virginia Theological Seminary and College." In 1924 she became librarian at a branch of the private Jones Memorial Library at

Dunbar High School, the only "colored" high school in segregated Lynchburg [fig. 6]. For over twenty years, for the meager salary of $75 a month, she introduced black high school students to the world of books, creating a series of interesting programs to engage their attention. She even supplemented the collection at Dunbar with her own books and lobbied successfully with the main branch of the Jones Memorial Library for more resources. A former Dunbar student, Christopher Edley, Sr., who went on to graduate from Harvard Law School and serve as president of the United Negro College Fund, recalled how Anne Spencer inspired him to read and helped lay the foundation for his career.[10]

In April of 1946 she retired as librarian and from that point forward was able to devote more time to her garden and poetry. From the 1920s onward, her home became a popular accommodation for African-American political leaders, and artists traveling between New York and Washington and Atlanta, and guest lecturers at the Virginia Theological Seminary. In segregated Virginia there were no public lodgings for African-American travelers or visitors. The Spencer household emerged as a lively salon, where such notables as Langston Hughes [fig. 7], Paul Robeson, W.E.B. Du Bois [fig. 8], Adam Clayton Powell, Jr., James Weldon Johnson, Countee Cullen, Sterling Brown, Thurgood Marshall, Marian Anderson, Zora Neale Hurston, George Washington Carver, Mary McLeod Bethune, Claude McKay, and the Reverend Martin Luther King, Jr. engaged in lively discussion, punctuated by refreshing strolls in the garden. Anne also traveled to New York, Washington, D.C., and Atlanta, where she became acquainted with many of the leading intellectuals of the Harlem Renaissance. The body of her published work was small, but of high quality, receiving many favorable reviews. After the death in 1938 of her dear friend James Weldon Johnson, who had aided her with the publication of many of her poems, she seemed to lose interest in publication. However, she continued to write poetry, producing hundreds of unpublished poems on scraps of paper and the inside covers of books. Much of this work has not survived.[11]

The last thirty years of Anne Spencer's life were a rich blend of

FIG. 1 *Anne Spencer in her garden, about 1925. Note the rich texture of the blooms and foliage.*

FIG. 2 *Edward and Anne Spencer with friends in the garden. Anne and Edward are at the far left of the photograph.*

FIG. 3 *Annie Bethel Scales Spencer in her wedding dress, May 15, 1901.*

FIG. 4 *Edward Alexander Spencer*

FIG. 5 *James Weldon Johnson*

FIG. 6 *Anne Spencer at Dunbar High School during her tenure as librarian.*

FIG. 7 *Langston Hughes*

FIG. 8 *W.E.B. Du Bois*

FIG. 9 *Anne Spencer in her later years.*

FIG. 10 *Spencer family portrait. Front row: Edward's parents and maternal grandparents with grandchildren. Back row: Edward at far left and his brother, Warwick, Jr., third from right, who later lived next door to Edward and Anne.*

FIG. 11 *Anne and Edward together in the garden, 1942.*

FIG. 12 *Anne and Edward in the sun porch at 1313 Pierce Street.*

political activity, entertaining, creative exploration, and personal cultivation [fig. 9]. She was constantly involved in various civil rights issues and was an outspoken critic of what she regarded as token desegregation of the local public schools. Her commitment was strengthened by what she described as "a colossal reserve of constructive indignation."[12] Edward's death in 1964 was a deep wound. Despite some serious health problems, she continued to write, to garden, to read, and to probe new ideas until her death on July 25, 1975. Well into her last year she was working on an unfinished epic poem, "A Dream of John Brown: On His Return Trip Home." Her last completed poem, "1975," she regarded as her "Antaeus," an affirmation that throughout her long life her strength had come from contact with the earth, like Antaeus, the formidable giant of Greek mythology. A firm believer in personal immortality, she looked forward to a reunion with Edward in the afterlife. They are buried together in a family plot in Lynchburg's Forest Hills Cemetery.

Anne's husband, Edward Alexander Spencer, was born in Lynchburg in 1876. The Spencer family [fig. 10] had acquired a considerable amount of land in the Pierce Street neighborhood, including the former Confederate Army campground that later became the site of the home Edward designed for his new wife. The family erected a neighborhood assembly hall, and, following the Civil War, offered lodging to freed slaves. Edward continued this tradition as a very generous and forgiving landlord and real-estate developer of Spencer Place, his private residential development. He also managed the family grocery store. Edward was also Lynchburg's first black parcel postman and was known for his gentle, affable spirit. As his son Chauncey remarked, "Mother was intense, but my father was a pleasure and a treasure." [figs. 11, 12][13] Over time he collected a rich assortment of architectural fragments, which, with Anne's consent, he incorporated into their house and garden. He supported Anne's efforts as a poet and hired household help to free her for the pursuit of her work. Together they traveled in the surrounding countryside to collect plants for Anne's garden, and he collaborated with her on its construction and maintenance. An amateur musician and landscape painter, and a devoted father and husband, Edward was a well-loved member of the community. He died May 17, 1964. The editorial page of the *Lynchburg News* praised him as "one of the city's most respected, exemplary citizens...generous, kindly, honorable and with a sensitive intelligence, such men live on in memory."[14]

A 1930s VISIT TO THE GARDEN

ANNE SPENCER'S GARDEN, LIKE HER POETRY, is subtle, original, richly nuanced, and carefully crafted. Her poetry often addressed life's contrasts and dichotomies. So did her garden. It was a place of both solitary retreat and social gathering. Its elements are a fusion of recycled architectural objects and high art garden designs. Throughout her life Spencer continually revised her poems. She reworked her garden in a similar manner—enlarging, re-crafting, and refining it over a period of seventy years.

As a young mother in the first decade of the 1900s, Anne planted a small vegetable garden adjacent to the back porch of her and Edward's new home.[15] In 1923 Anne, with Edward's help, expanded her garden dramatically to encompass an area stretching from the back porch of their house all the way to Buchanan Street, which bordered the rear of their property. The garden now was a narrow rectangle approximately 40 feet wide and 195 feet long. Edward constructed 3-ft. high retaining walls on the northwest corner to level the site and installed water lines to supply the garden pools. In 1924 Edward built Edankraal, Anne's cottage study. The three-car garage adjacent to it was later demolished [fig. 13], and the vegetable garden was removed. This enlargement of Anne's garden was emblematic of her expanding career as a poet. Her first poems had been published nationally in the early 1920s, and the construction of her cottage study shortly thereafter bore witness to her deep commitment to her vocation as a poet. The new garden was an economic luxury as well, since it encompassed a vacant residential lot at the rear of the house, which would have sold for a handsome price in the rapidly developing neighborhood. The expanded garden soon gained the admiration of Anne's family and many friends and visitors.

From the 1920s on Anne continued to enrich the plant palette and architectural detail of her garden. We lack detailed information on the exact sequence of construction. Family photographs suggest that soon after the construction of Edankraal a large wisteria pergola was built next to it [fig. 14]. Over the next seven or so years Anne added several new elements most likely in the following sequence: a circular pool with a fountain and semicircular bench at the far end of the garden [fig. 15], two paths along the sides of the garden [fig. 16], and one down the center. Finally, she erected a grape arbor that subdivided the long narrow space between the pergola and the pool at the far end of the garden [fig. 17]. Anne's planting plan also changed over time. At first she planted the entire area stretching from the pergola to the pool with a lush and colorful bed of annual and perennial flowers and roses [figs. 18, 19]. After she subdivided this long space she retained the lush flowerbed in the section between the pergola and the new grape arbor but removed the flowers from the area around the pool. Her revised planting plan for the pool area was more understated and spatially sophisticated. She created an intimate garden room defined by clipped privet hedges, lawn, and Virginia red cedars centering on the pool. The lawn was enlivened with a scattering of ornamental evergreen trees and flowering dogwoods [fig. 20].

By the end of the 1930s she had completed the garden's basic structure, which included her cottage study, a pool and fountain, three paths, a pergola, a grape arbor, a new gate, and flowerbeds. The garden reached its zenith in the fifteen or so years after the Second World War. During this period Anne had ceased to work as librarian at Dunbar High School and her three children had completed their education, married, and moved elsewhere. Now she had ample time to devote to the care of her garden and to experiment with new and more elaborate plant palettes. From the 1960s until her death in 1975, the inevitable infirmities of old age compromised her later efforts and her garden, that most fragile and temporal of all arts, suffered. What we visit today is a carefully researched and sensitive restoration, carried out in the early 1980s. It differs in some aspects from Anne's original garden depicted in family photos from the late 1930s and early 1940s. Just how will be discussed in a later section since the restoration deserves its own story.

In what follows, let us attempt to visualize the garden as it would have appeared in the late 1930s since this period is the one most extensively documented in family photographs and represents one of the garden's high points. This is the garden we would have experienced had we been guests at one of the Spencers' typical gatherings of artists and intellectuals, some members of the Harlem Renaissance, others from the local college community, who used the garden as a kind of lively outdoor salon. A note of caution is necessary. A few tiles of our garden mosaic are missing, but numerous family photos and the sharp memories of Chauncey Spencer and his wife Anne allow us a close approximation.

On our visit in the late 1930s, Anne's garden presents us with an array of subtle and engaging features. It appears as four well-defined rooms [fig. 21] enlivened by a lush and colorful palette of plants and imaginatively recycled architectural fragments. She threads her garden on a central axis like the unified structure of her poems, yet avoids monotony through rich variety and asymmetry. She skillfully uses a pergola and a grape arbor to frame views and create thresholds and transitions. Her crisply delineated gravel paths have begun to replace earlier ones constructed of turf. They lead us on diagonals and semicircles, providing ever-changing views and long vistas down corridors of bloom [fig. 22]. Her garden invites us to choose, perhaps a powerful metaphor for life's choices and opportunities for exploration within limited boundaries. It embodies strength and delicacy, discipline and spontaneity. Quiet pools flavor the garden with serenity and invite solitary reflection or relaxed conversation with friends. She offers us places to stroll and places to linger, as well as inviting shade and warming sun. She deliberately chooses certain plants to attract birds to enliven the garden with song and aerial acrobatics. This garden, just as a sixteenth-century Chinese scholar's garden, appears much larger through the rich spatial and sensual experiences it offers.

Anne's garden reveals the vitality and bold experimentation of the self-taught designer that she was. Her design work appears to nod a bit in the direction of the plans and details for "small residential gardens" in her extensive collection of popular garden magazines of the 1920s and 30s, *Country Life*, *Garden and Home Builder* [fig. 23], *Better*

Homes and Gardens, *House Beautiful*, *The American Home*, and *House and Garden*.[16] Here we find axial order, clearly defined rooms, and lush English cottage garden planting somewhat similar to Anne's garden [figs. 24, 25, 26, 27]. Yet Anne's garden is far more than a highly competent rephrasing of the popular small-scale residential gardens of the 20s and 30s. Her work is infused with vitality and color through her artful collage of salvaged architectural fragments such as stained glass windows [fig. 28], ornate turned wooden columns [fig. 29], and delicate cast iron fence details [fig. 30]. Edward had gathered these from friends and clients on his parcel post delivery rounds, and Anne had repainted many of them in vivid sea foam green and robin's egg blue, two of her favorite colors. The tightly restrained details of *Better Homes and Gardens* or *Country Life*'s "favorite garden of the month" pale in comparison to Anne's exuberant experiments. Her planting style is a bold and flamboyant combination of colors and textures. She avoids the single-color garden rooms so popular in the garden literature of the 1920s and 30s.

Certain features in Anne's garden resemble those of rural African-American vernacular gardens. These include her imaginative improvisations with recycled materials, use of brilliant floral color, and the skillful inclusion of plants gathered from the wild. Also in the tradition of rural vernacular gardens, she celebrates family and community by sharing her garden on occasion with her extended family, friends, and neighbors. Another common trait is Anne's practice of sustainable gardening through carefully enriching her soil with organic materials. However, members of Anne's immediate family do not recall her mentioning any influence of rural African-American gardening traditions on her work. She always affirmed she had discovered gardening after her marriage and was proud of being self-taught in its art and craft. She noted her mother had no interest in gardens. Also, there is no evidence in her autobiographical remarks to her biographer, J. Lee Greene, that gardens attracted her interest while growing up in Bramwell, although she did recall her love of exploring the surrounding forests and streams. Perhaps these echoes of African-American vernacular traditions were part of Edward's design sensitivity, which influenced Anne's work.[17] In any case, her garden with its rich and original combination of vivid colors, architectural fragments, and lushly planted, well-proportioned garden rooms presents us with a sophisticated, original, and delightful work of garden art. Its many fine qualities invite a closer look.

The treatment of the front of the house along Pierce Street deserves our attention before examining the garden in the rear. A low privet hedge provides a sense of separation from the street, yet does not interfere with conversations from the veranda with neighbors passing by on their evening promenades. The floor plan of the understated Queen Anne house [fig. 31] designed by Edward, who also supervised its construction, is straightforward and functional. Its elegant two-bay façade with a recessed section is topped by a hipped roof. The front veranda changes into a rose-covered pergola on the west façade. The first floor contains an entry vestibule, living room [fig. 32], dining room, kitchen, and sun porch; the second floor, family and guest bedrooms, and a bathroom; the third floor was later remodeled as a bedroom for their grandchildren.[18] The vivid maroons, blues, and greens of the living room, guestrooms, and dining room are echoed in the garden. The bold textures of framed panels of wallpaper are repeated outdoors in strong foliage combinations. Edward incorporated salvaged architectural fragments, such as stained glass windows and mirrors, in the interior of the house, just as he did in the garden.

The black and gray checkerboard pattern of the concrete entry walk creates a bold and inviting path to the veranda, which is paved in the same manner [fig. 33]. Anne provides seasonal color with a mixed planting of dogwoods and hydrangeas and a large Climbing American Beauty rosebush that cascades over the pergola on the west side of the house. The overall effect of this front yard is of quiet simplicity and elegance. If we stroll down the driveway, we encounter another stroke of Anne's originality. Rather than constructing the typical and unsightly bed of asphalt or concrete, Anne designed a paving pattern of 16-inch brick strips to support car wheels set in an expanse of grassy lawn [fig. 34].

We begin our imaginary 1930s garden walk at the immediate rear of the house where we encounter the first garden room, featuring flowers, especially roses. This unfenced area is a lush tapestry of vivid colors.

Anne preferred bold combinations of colors, as both her garden and the interior of the house reveal. This first garden room opens to the adjacent yard of Edward's brother Warwick, where a croquet pitch affords lively family entertainment [fig. 35]. Anne's garden, although a private realm, is also part of a living arrangement that includes the couple's extended family. This first garden room, and indeed the entire garden itself, is closely linked to the interior of the house. It is clearly visible from the elevated two-story rear porch, which was later enclosed to form additional rooms [fig. 36]. Towering some twenty-one feet above the garden room on a slender iron pole is a purple martin house, one of several in the garden [fig. 37]. The martins' annual northward migration to summer quarters in Lynchburg is a cherished harbinger of spring and provides welcome assistance in controlling insects, especially the voracious mosquitoes who visit on balmy summer evenings.

Anne's latticed, robin's egg blue gate at the end of the first garden room provides us with a colorful entry to the second room at the garden's heart, the cottage garden.[19] This gate is another example of imaginative recycling since it is constructed from the old latticework of the remodeled back porch [fig. 38]. Tucked alongside the west border of this second garden room is Anne's one-room shingle-clad cottage, her private sanctuary [fig. 39]. The entry porch of this small vernacular building is turned to the short width of the garden so Anne can gaze down the full length of her garden through the window directly above her writing desk, along the south wall [fig. 40]. The cottage's name, "Edankraal," blends her and Edward's names with "kraal," the Afrikaans word for "dwelling" [fig. 41]. The first two syllables also refer to the biblical Garden of Eden, a very appropriate pun since this indeed is Anne's cherished Eden, the symbolic center of a garden nurturing creativity and bonds of friendship. Edankraal's vivid sea foam green columns, stained glass window, and Gothic wire screens are recycled from demolished houses in Lynchburg. A clever native greenstone chimney serves as a flue for both the grill on the exterior used for family cookouts and the small woodstove on the interior. Attached to the chimney near its top is a large metal "S". A small square planting bed in front of the cottage is a mosaic of colorful miniature flowers. Interior

FIG. 13 *An early view of the garden showing Anne Spencer's study, Edankraal, and the three-car garage.*

FIG. 14 *The pergola abundant with wisteria blooms. Note the ornate turned wooden post.*

FIG. 15 *Anne Spencer and a friend at the newly completed pool. Note the Prince Ebo fountain at the lower right and the unplanted garden area behind.*

FIG. 16 *Turf path on the east side of the garden. The unplanted area in fig. 15 has now been extensively planted with perennials, annuals and roses.*

FIG. 17 *Spencer children and friends in front of the grape arbor.*

FIG. 18 *View of the garden from the fountain toward the house. Note the absence of the grape arbor and the lush planting extending from the pool to the pergola.*

FIG. 19 *View of the garden looking backward toward the fountain. The planting plan of this area was later revised substantially. The head of Prince Ebo is visible at the edge of the pool.*

FIG. 20 *A view of the pool area in 1937, showing the revised planting plan. Note the privet hedges, lawn and cedars. Anne and Edward are seated by the pool.*

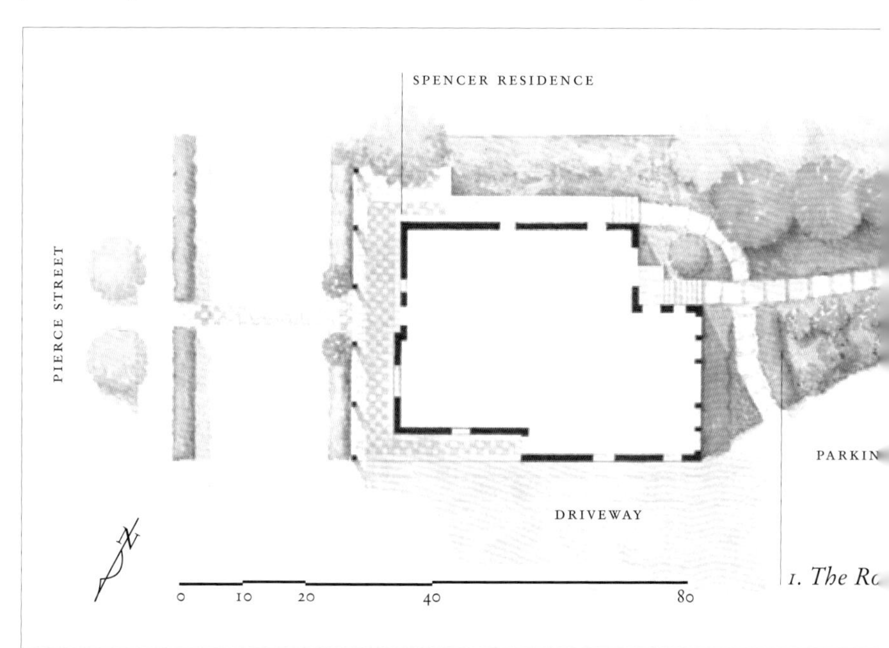

FIG. 21 *A plan of the restored garden. The site encompasses two residential lots.*

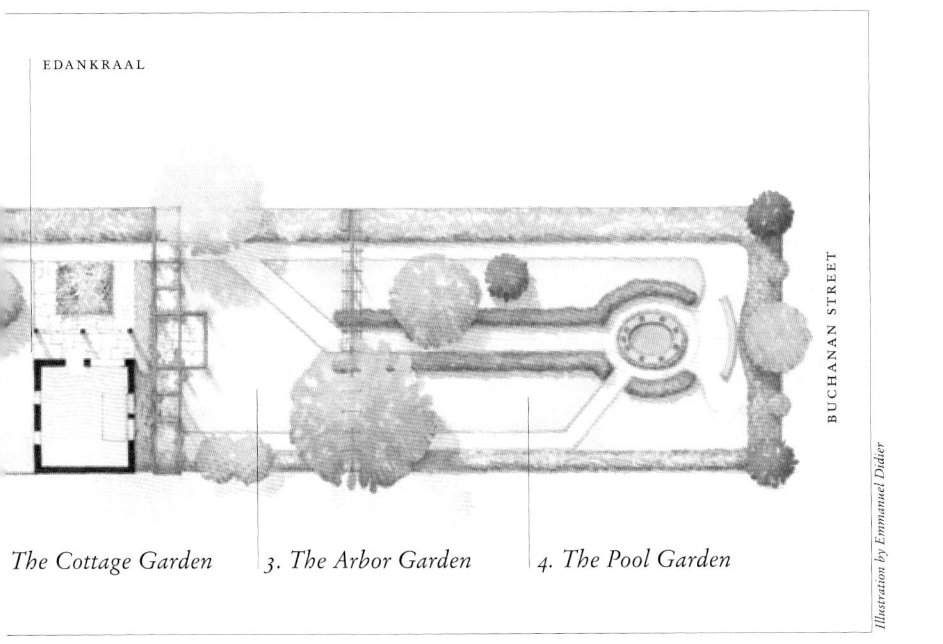

Illustration by Emmanuel Didier

FIG. 22 *Anne Spencer in her garden about 1940. The planting beds in the third garden room are divided by a turf path. Note the purple martin house in the background.*

furnishings are functional and modest: a small sleeping cot, bookshelves, easy chairs, and a writing desk. A good luck horseshoe is nailed above the threshold. Here in this intimate setting, surrounded by photographs of family and friends and her extensive library of British, American, and European poetry and history, Anne composes her poetry.

A third, adjacent garden room just beyond Edankraal is framed by a wisteria pergola on the north end and a grape arbor on the south. The pergola, grape arbor, and nearby Edankraal are all painted in the rich brownish-red of the main house, creating a skillful linkage of house and garden. The four sides of the pergola [fig. 42] are expanded to form a small room with simple backless seats in the four corners [fig. 43]. Here is an intimate nook for reading or conversation with a pleasing view down the main axis. In the center of the square pergola is a small circular pool, to be later replaced by a cast plaster and concrete statue of Minerva, the Roman goddess of wisdom, the gift of a friend who wanted to honor Anne's intellect and creativity [fig. 44]. Continuing past the pergola, three paths invite us to stroll through this third garden room, and Anne flares the center path on a bold diagonal, a deft touch of asymmetry that adds variety and a shift of view [fig. 45]. Anne plants the floor of this room from edge to edge with a lush tapestry of many varieties of flowers, some of which have been mail-ordered from nursery catalogs. Her bold combinations of color provide continuous bloom for many months of the growing season. The wooden grape arbor at the far end of this third room marks its end but also is the threshold to the serene pool garden, the fourth and last garden room, a skillfully designed climax to her garden's processional paths. The three rectangular portals of the grape arbor frame views into the pool garden like paintings arranged in a gallery [fig. 46].

Anne's pool garden is a quiet space for conversation and reflection, and it draws us like a magnet. In this room Anne works with plants alone to define space; there are no additional pergolas or arbors. She chooses as its main feature a circular room of greenery walled by privet hedges and taller columnar Virginia red cedars. Anne extends the lower privet hedges along the center path and the flanking side paths leading to this circular sanctuary [fig. 20]. On the south side a large vase-shaped deutzia arches over the space, completing its ceiling, buffering an unattractive view of a factory to the south. It also provides striking white blossoms in late May, which fall like snow upon the ground below [fig. 47]. Anne defined the center of this room with the most elaborate pool of the garden. Its circular form is surrounded by a vivid sea green and maroon concrete frame and features a central spray fountain. Languidly spewing a small stream of water into the waterlily-clad pool is the cast iron head of an African prince, a work of the Ebo tribe of West Africa. This was a gift of W.E.B. Du Bois, the distinguished author and political leader who had purchased it on a trip to Africa. Anne dubbed him "Prince Ebo" [figs. 48, 49]. Beneath Prince Ebo's gaze colorful goldfish animate the pond.

The entire floor of this final garden room is lawn, interspersed with a few small dogwoods and evergreens [fig. 20]. Like many Virginia Piedmont gardens, it especially celebrates the bloom of the long, balmy spring, which Anne captured so well in her witty poem, "Life-Long, Poor Browning":

> Here canopied reaches of dogwood and hazel,
> Beech tree and redbud fine-laced in vines,
> Fleet clapping rills by lush fern and basil,
> Drain blue hills to lowlands scented with pines...[20]

The crisp geometry of the privet hedges and the simple planting palette of this fourth room form a vivid contrast to the field of bright colors that enveloped us as we crossed the adjacent third room.

A gently curving sea green concrete bench, which echoes the form of the pool, invites us to sit beneath the deutzia's canopy, near the pool. The bench, identical in color to the posts of Edankraal, is wide enough to hold a picnic and long enough to accommodate a small gathering of friends. From here we can view the full length of the garden along its central axis [fig. 48]. Three of the garden rooms are enclosed with a transparent wire mesh fence topped with lacy cast iron trim reclaimed from the old fence of Lynchburg's Randolph-Macon Woman's College [figs. 30, 35]. Anne plants the fence line with shrubs and old-fashioned flowers, a welcome screen from the work-a-day world. The deep shadows of her garden's tree canopy alternate with bands of bright sunlight. Birdsong and fragrance abound as a complement to the quiet voice of the fountain. Edankraal, discreetly tucked to the side of the main axis, emerges from the shade as an inviting retreat, and the Spencers' house recedes as a far distant realm beyond the garden's edge. The elegant concentric circles of the pool and its semi-circular bench and hedge suggest a sense of gathering, a gathering of friends and family as well as of one's inner resources. We are present in a true poet's garden, a place of delight, metamorphosis, centering, and renewal.

ROUTINES AND RITUALS IN THE GARDEN

A GARDEN IS A TAPESTRY OF RELATIONSHIPS between those who design and care for the garden, those who visit and appreciate it, and the garden itself. Anne Spencer's daily routine was interwoven with her garden. Over the course of her long life, her activities inevitably varied, but the one constant was her ongoing participation in the maintenance and enjoyment of her garden. Chauncey Spencer and his wife Anne related a story of the poet's morning ritual in the years after her retirement as librarian at Dunbar High School: she would arise late, never hurrying, and begin the day standing by the window of her second story sleeping porch, brushing her hair and gazing down into the garden, often for as long as an hour.[21] This daily practice gave Anne the opportunity to gather her thoughts, center her soul, and plan the day before her. Her garden's beauty offered a visual meditation with which to start each day.

Although the garden was considered to be Anne's, the maintenance of the garden was shared by Anne and Edward.[22] Only rarely did they hire help, as Anne was a perfectionist and wanted to maintain maximum control over the design and the cultivation of her garden. Two trusted gardeners were employed on occasion, Mr. Teague and Mr. Ragland. Occasionally the children were asked to help. Chauncey Spencer remembered that he was instructed to weed out only the easily identifiable weeds such as dandelion and chickweed. With an extensive herbaceous palette, the garden chores were many. But the maintenance of the garden was a pleasure for Anne [fig. 50]. Often she continued her work on into the evening by the light of the moon or with the addition of candles. Especially during the heat and humidity of summer, the Spencers extended their daily enjoyment of the garden's pleasures into the evening [fig. 11]. Gardening was a daily activity throughout the week, but on Sundays Anne and Edward varied the routine by driving together out into the surrounding countryside, where they collected wildflowers and native trees and shrubs for the garden. They would sometimes travel great distances in search of a horticultural treasure. The love for gardening was a shared joy. The reputation of Anne Spencer's garden spread far over the years. In his introduction to the group of Anne's poems in *The Book of American Negro Poetry*, James Weldon Johnson wrote, "She lives in Lynchburg and takes great pride and pleasure in the cultivation of her beautiful garden."[23] Anne delighted in such praise and the garden became increasingly more elaborate and refined in response to admiration. The garden's reputation attracted many visitors, including local amateur painters.

Both Edward and Anne Spencer enjoyed entertaining their distinguished out-of-town guests. Frequently gatherings began in the house, with food, music, and conversation. Chauncey Spencer told about sitting with his sisters on the steps above the living room, watching Paul Robeson sing "My Little Gal": "It was what we used to call in my days of jazz 'a jam session'—a jam session of poetry and art and so forth."[24] Parties often continued out into the garden, sometimes late into the evening. The variety of garden paths, separated from each other by lush planting, provided places to stroll and converse in private. The large curved bench at the very end of the garden made an appealing place to sit quietly or engage in conversation. Family photographs show friends and distinguished guests gathered in the garden. In addition to out-of-town guests, neighbors also visited the garden regularly, grateful for the opportunity to enjoy its captivating beauty. Chauncey Spencer described his mother's garden as "the proud possession of the neighborhood."[25]

Anne had strong opinions about the limits of her garden hospitality. On one occasion a neighbor remarked on the abundance of grapes growing in the garden, and asked permission to pick some. Anne denied this request, saying that because the birds provided the insect control in the garden she would save all the grapes as their reward. Anne was reluctant even to pick flowers from the garden, lest this diminish the garden's effect. Chauncey's wife, Anne, recalls how the poet would send her to visit an ailing neighbor with a tiny get-well bouquet of miniature blossoms, "but that was all!"[26]

The Spencers loved to watch the birds and were grateful for the animation that birds added to the garden. They planted corn to fill the numerous birdfeeders throughout the garden. Birdsong was constant and pleasing. Anne and Edward's pet crow, Joe [fig. 51], who had a vocabulary of between twenty-five and thirty words, entertained guests with his antics and was well known throughout the neighborhood.

The only foods grown for humans were parsley, mint, and fruit from the apple and pear trees. Anne's garden was clearly a horticultural endeavor, not an agricultural one, and it was planted for beauty, not for harvest. Anne Spencer created her garden as an ideal world unto itself, a sanctuary to nurture and sustain herself, her family, her neighbors, and her friends.

The garden continued to provide the site for numerous gatherings, both formal and casual, over the course of the many years it flourished [fig. 52]. Although it did not include spaces large enough for sports, her family and their friends often enjoyed croquet or badminton in the adjacent garden of their cousins [fig. 35]. Players later would return to Anne's garden for refreshments and conversation. Anne was an avid card-player and Edankraal was a popular place for bridge and other card games. Family celebrations were held in the garden [fig. 53], including the weddings of Anne's second daughter, Alroy, and her granddaughter, Chauncey's daughter, Shaun.

Throughout her life, Anne was especially interested in nurturing and encouraging children [fig. 17]. When the Spencer children were young, they were members of Jack and Jill clubs, a national network of social organizations for the enrichment of African-American youth. The local clubs held weekly meetings in the garden. Anne also provided lessons in etiquette for young boys and girls to help prepare them for their later professional careers. As a librarian and teacher, Anne Spencer mourned the scarcity of good reading material for children and she encouraged friends such as W.E.B. Du Bois to promote children's literature.[27] As a gardener and parent, Anne always welcomed the friends of her children and grandchildren into the garden [fig. 54]. As an old woman, she often invited groups of school children for conversations and discussions. Always the thoughtful hostess, she would instruct her cook, Mrs. Meekins, to prepare miniature hamburgers and small pieces of hotdogs for the children to barbecue on Edankraal's grill. In April of 1972, several years before she died, Anne Spencer wrote an open letter to young people who might be interested in her life and her poetry. It is a whimsical piece, light-hearted and a bit nonsensical, but at the core of the letter, couched in gardener's terminology, is Anne's deepest belief:

> Thankfully, as we grow we sprout whatever aptitudes each one owns as a life-gift.... What I'm trying to beg of you is use your gift—if it's a true one it will have meaning for you and every life yours touches.[28]

Anne Spencer's own life-gift was her garden, through which she touched the lives of many neighbors, friends, and family members until the end of her life.

While Anne's garden served as an important place of social gathering, its primary role was to provide her with the creative solitude critical to her work. During the twenty-one years Anne Spencer worked full time as a librarian, she planned her daily routine to allow for much time in her garden. When she returned home from school each day, she would go out into the garden with a tray of dinner prepared by Mrs. Meekins, and she often remained there until two or three in the morning, long after the family was asleep. Sometimes she would sleep on the small cot in Edankraal. Here she could gather her thoughts, compose her poems, and take in the inspiration and restorative ambience of the natural world, especially necessary after a long day of work. After she retired as librarian in 1946, the garden enjoyed "its greatest splendor,"[29] flourishing with the attention both Anne and Edward were able to lavish on it. Following Edward's death in 1964, Anne's travels, ill health, and failing energy curtailed her garden activities somewhat. When limited to her house, Anne chose to spend her days in her first floor sunroom, which afforded good views out into the garden. She was still involved with her garden through the daily observation and appreciation of its ever-changing beauty. This routine was a source of joy and solace to Anne Spencer for over seventy-two years.

Illustration by F. William Haemmal

FIG. 23 *A garden magazine from Anne Spencer's personal collection. Note the color plan for a small-scale residential garden.*

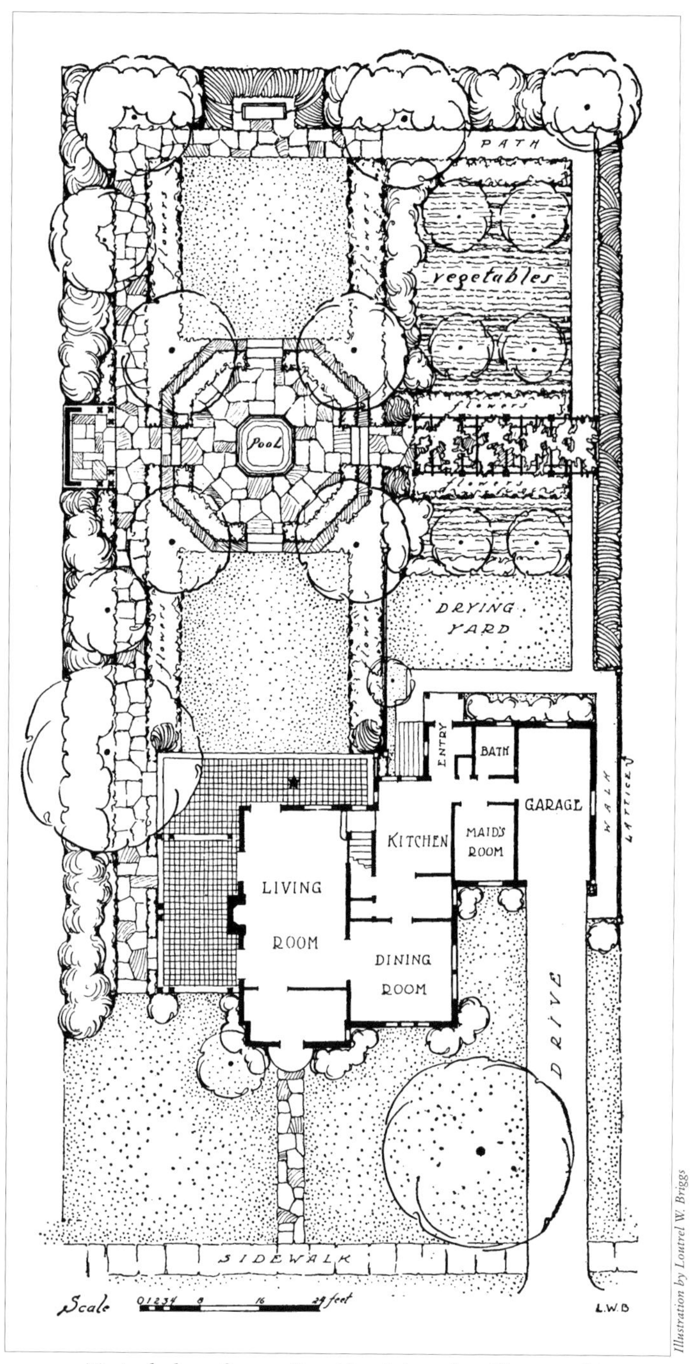

Illustration by Loutrel W. Briggs

FIG. 24 *Typical plan of a small residential garden, illustrated in* GARDEN & HOME BUILDER, *January 1926. The lush floral borders and strong axial plan are reminiscent of Anne Spencer's garden [fig. 21].*

Illustration by Loutrel W. Briggs

FIG. 25 *Perspective drawing of the plan in fig. 24. The placement of the bench at the end of the main axis is similar to Anne Spencer's garden [fig. 21].*

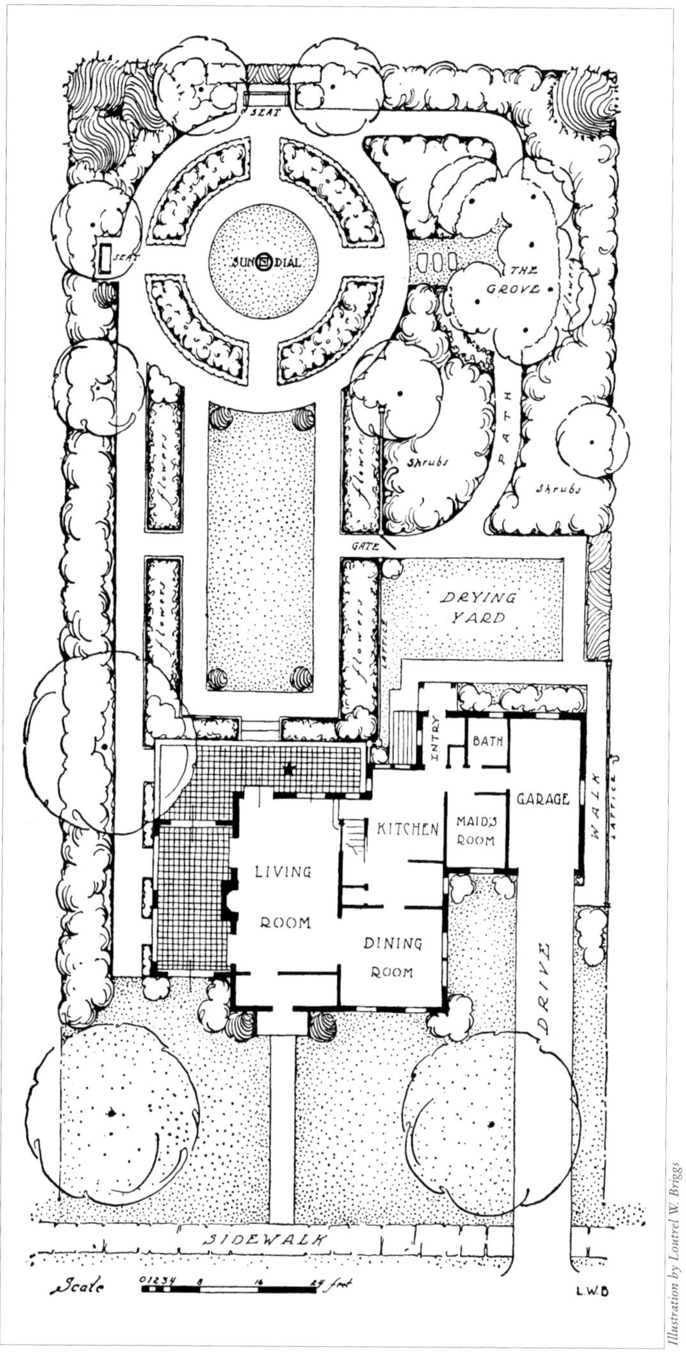

Illustration by Loutrel W. Briggs

FIG. 26 *An alternative plan of the garden in fig. 24. Note the resemblance in spatial organization and scale to Anne Spencer's garden, illustrated in fig. 21.*

Illustration by Loutrel W. Briggs

FIG. 27 *Perspective drawing of the plan in fig. 26. The circular area around the sundial is reminiscent of Anne Spencer's pool garden, depicted in fig. 48.*

FIG. 28 *The view from Anne Spencer's desk in Edankraal through the recycled stained glass window.*

FIG. 29 *A recycled wooden column supporting the porch of Edankraal, viewed through another recycled element, a Gothic wire screen.*

FIG. 30 *Cast iron fence trim reclaimed from the old fence at Randolph-Macon Woman's College.*

FIG. 31 *1313 Pierce Street, the house Edward Spencer built for his new wife in 1903.*

THE GARDEN AS THE POET'S MUSE

ANNE SPENCER'S POETRY AND HER GARDEN reveal the selfsame creative spirit.[30] Gardens provide the settings for many of her poems, inspiration for her work, and many of her most powerful images and metaphors. Experience with her own garden offered the grounding from which her expressions of ideas could take flight. In a short untitled poem, she writes,

> Earth, I thank you
> for the pleasure of your language
> You've had a hard time
> bringing it to me
> from the ground
> to grunt thru the noun
> To all the way
> feeling seeing smelling touching
> —awareness
> I am here![31]

The message is inescapable: the garden is the wellspring of her creative powers. The earth speaks directly through the voice of the poet.

Anne Spencer wrote poetry from her childhood until shortly before her death. She published her first poem in the journal of the NAACP, *The Crisis*, in 1920, at the age of 38. She was included in anthologies such as James Weldon Johnson's *The Book of American Negro Poetry* (1922), Alain Locke's *The New Negro* (1925), and Countee Cullen's *Caroling Dusk: An Anthology of Verse by Negro Poets* (1927). She published in various periodicals through 1931. In 1949, when she was 67 years old, her last published poem appeared in *The Poetry of the Negro, 1746-1949*, edited by Langston Hughes and

Arna Bontemps. Although Spencer told her biographer that she had written "a thousand or so" poems, only twenty were published during her lifetime.[32] Publication was not essential to Anne Spencer's commitment to her poetry. On the occasion of her ninetieth birthday, she declared,

> I never sent one of my poems away to sell but I certainly did get hooked up with a lot of people in the publishing business. I was smart about my work, though. I never gave it to a real critic, only my dearest friends who loved me very much...[33]

Throughout her life Anne Spencer wrote for her own satisfaction, and revisions to her earlier poems were ongoing. In 1972, she changed one word in the title of her first published poem, "Before the Feast of Shushan, " replacing "of" with "at." And at the age of 91 she continued to refine and polish one of her favorite poems, "Substitution," first published in 1927 when she was 45. Spencer wrote her final poem when she was 92, one year before her death. Her long life as a poet was an ongoing quest.

Jessie Redmon Fauset, literary editor of *The Crisis* from 1919-1926, aptly described Anne Spencer's work as "true and fine; she blends a delicate mysticism with a diamond clearness of exposition."[34] Anne Spencer's poetry was a journey into the realms of truth and beauty. A major guide in this search was the Transcendentalist philosopher and poet, Ralph Waldo Emerson. In her writing we can see considerable evidence of the inspiration Spencer discovered in Emerson, for whom nature was the source of insight, joy, and solace, and the beauty of nature an expression of the presence of God. Anne Spencer chose to follow Emerson's advice that the individual follow his own path, imitating no one but pursuing a life of philosophical exploration. In Emerson's *Nature*, Anne Spencer read,

> The lover of nature is he whose inward and outward senses are still truly adjusted to each other; who has retained the spirit of infancy even into the era of manhood. His intercourse with heaven and earth

> becomes part of his daily food. In the presence of nature a wild delight runs through the man, in spite of real sorrows....Not the sun or the summer alone, but every hour and season yields its tribute of delight....Within these plantations of God, a decorum and sanctity reign....There I feel that nothing can befall me in life—no disgrace, no calamity...which nature cannot repair....The currents of the Universal Being circulate through me; I am part and parcel of God.[35]

Emerson wrote too of the importance of solitude, and the fact that this essential element of creativity cannot always be found in a room full of books and letters, even when one is alone. He advised the writer to find calm and quiet, beauty and inspiration in the natural world. For Anne Spencer daily time outdoors in her garden was crucial to her creative process.

As a poet, Anne Spencer discovered inspiration in a wide variety of literary sources, individuals, and traditions in addition to Emerson.[36] Her education at Virginia Seminary had given her a good background in both Christian doctrine and biblical literature. Similarly she had studied the Greek and Roman classics and found therein a valuable source of images and symbols. Spencer's desire for knowledge was voracious, and she employed numerous and varied resources in her search for information and ideas. Her 1928 *Funk & Wagnall's New Standard Dictionary* still includes numerous bookmarks, including one indicating a page entitled "A Partial List of Flowers and their Symbolic Meanings." She read widely in the work of other poets, among whom her favorite was Robert Browning. James Weldon Johnson referred her to the poems of Gerard Manley Hopkins, and Spencer acquired a volume of his work for her extensive library. Both her home and her garden study, Edankraal, are overflowing with volumes of history and nineteenth- and twentieth-century American, English, and European poetry, and many of these are stuffed with scraps of paper with Spencer's observations, ideas, and responses. Her marginalia provide a valuable glimpse into what the poet was thinking and how her ideas took shape.

Apparently her process of composition was slow and thoughtful, and was engaged inextricably in the meditative routines of her gardening. She told J. Lee Greene, her biographer, "How I make a poem. I start with a word or two and begin associating."[37] This "associating" might continue for many years. Anne Spencer did not write for praise or publication; she was hesitant to share her work. She composed poetry for her own satisfaction and as an exploration, parallel to that of her ongoing garden adventure, into the expression of her creative spirit [fig. 55]. She once remarked to Countee Cullen, "I write about some of the things I love. But have no civilized articulation for the things I hate."[38] At least seventeen of her forty-three extant poems relate to the garden. Spencer deals with other topics as well, but as an object of focus garden themes and garden imagery predominate. While Spencer did not envision her poems in neat categories, it is helpful to consider the role of the garden in her work in several overlapping themes.

The Garden as Inspiration

Specific details of the garden provided inspiration, as valuable sources of ideas and images with which the poet's lyrical wanderings might begin. Three poems choose a specific garden plant as a point of departure. "Lines to a Nasturtium," subtitled parenthetically "A Lover Muses," is spoken directly to the flower, the poet's favorite [fig. 56].[39] She asks the blossom:

> Flame-flower, Day-torch, Mauna Loa,
> I saw a daring bee, today, pause, and soar,
> Into your flaming heart;
> Then did I hear crisp, crinkled laughter
> As the furies after tore him apart?[40]

Spencer celebrates the seductive beauty of the bloom, comparing it to a lover, "one other to whom you are in beauty born in vain." She uses her observations of the dramas of sexual attraction in the world of nature to deepen her passionate description of a human relationship. She concludes,

Ah, how the sense reels at my repeating,
As once in her fire-lit heart I felt the furies
Beating, beating.

The world of the garden is anything but tame; the words of the poet are scarcely restrained.

In "Grapes: Still-Life," Spencer again addresses a plant in her garden in a poem of many layers of meaning. In six stanzas, she speaks to three different grape varieties, Niagara, Caco, and Concord [fig. 57]. She examines the fruits closely, describing their flower structure, the color and substance of the fruit, and the symbolism of their names. She then uses these varying qualities of the grapes as a point of departure from which to explore deeper issues of race and heritage, symbolized by the grapes' differences.

You green-white Niagara,
Cool dull Nordic of your kind,—
Does your thick meat flinch
From these... touch and press your rind?

...
Concord, the too peaceful one
Purpling at your side,
All the colors of his flask
Holding high in pride...[41]

The poet intensifies the power of the poem by contrasting these fruits of the garden, typically evocative of a peaceful, Edenic world, with a world wracked by racial tension, symbolized in one example by the light-skinned, "Nordic" Niagara "flinching" from the darker, "purpling" Concord. In the poem's opening lines the grapes are "sweet globes, aged essence of the sun." By the last stanza the Niagara grape is "you who force the plight," a clear reference to racial discord. The poem ends with a strong affirmation of the shared humanity of all races symbolized by the identical "root" of all three grapes; their differences are only surface ones. Addressing the "Nordic" Niagara grape, Spencer affirms:

> This, too, is your heritage,
> You who force the plight;
> Blood and bone you turn to them
> For their root is white.

The poet travels a journey of discovery, through a land of pain. The plant is inspiration and symbol; the poetic investigation is deep and searching.

A third poem, "Creed," employs this device of the garden as point of departure for a series of reflections on human behavior and its theological implications. The poem begins,

> If my garden oak spares one bare ledge
> For a boughed mistletoe to grow and wedge;
> And all the wild birds this year should know
> I cherish their freedom to come and go;[42]

These four lines present the first of four situations that reveal evidence of compassion, trust, charity, or understanding on this earth. The second such situation describes a stray dog and a young boy, each trusting in the compassion of the speaker. In the third, the poet presents first a friend, then a foe, each acknowledging her generosity and understanding. The fourth example of charity and love describes human interaction with the speaker, ranging from a wandering pilgrim to a beloved husband. The last two lines, a final rhyming couplet, complete the musing:

> I may challenge God when we meet That Day,
> And He dare not be silent or send me away.

The poet anticipates Judgment Day, it seems, as a moment of confrontation. Perhaps proof of so much compassion in the human and natural world suggests God will manifest the same generosity and understanding on Judgment Day and listen to the challenges of the speaker? Although the poem does not reveal the substance of that challenge and we do not know whether this piece is autobiographical, it is clear that a simple observation in the garden initiates a series of probing meditations.

The Garden as Painful Reality

This method of using the garden as a point of departure can be seen in other poems, including a poem based on a work of Robert Browning entitled "Any Wife to Any Husband: A Derived Poem." The poet employs the metaphor of the garden and specifically the relationship between the garden and the gardener as a means of speculating about a possible future connection with a husband after the death of his wife. The poem reads,

> This small garden is half my world
> I am nothing to it—when all is said,
> I plant the thorn and kiss the rose,
> But they will grow when I am dead.
>
> Let not this change, Love, the human life
> Share with her the joy you had with me,
> List with her the plaintive bird you heard with me.
> Feel all human joys, but
> Feel most "a shadowy third."[43]

The poet invites the reader to eavesdrop on a meditation that is taking place in a garden. This poem also recognizes one of the poignant truths of gardening: the garden as an entity will endure, albeit in a different state of maintenance, long after the death of its caretaker. The garden is a stage on which dramas of deterioration, death, and rebirth occur. The gardener's hopes often feel futile, and an inexperienced gardener soon realizes that she has far less control over her garden than she might like. The garden brings us to a point of recognition, if not acceptance, of some of life's harsh realities.

Spencer paints this metaphor of the garden in a particularly somber palette in a short untitled and unpublished piece that reads,

> God never planted a garden
> But He placed a keeper there;
> And the keeper ever razed the ground
> And built a city where
> God cannot walk at the eve of day,
> Nor take the morning air.[44]

The poet refers to the Garden of Eden with considerable poetic license. In the original account in Genesis, God created a garden and placed within it two humans. They did not destroy the garden directly, but neither did they protect and preserve it. Their disobedience to God caused their expulsion from the garden and led their offspring to create a violent and chaotic world of evil cities.[45] Here Spencer goes beyond the biblical account and associates sinful humanity with the actual destruction of the Garden of Eden itself. For her this single garden symbolizes the entire world, and metaphorically the message is clear. The finality of this piece reveals powerfully a despair that often colored Spencer's moods. However, this grim spirit provides breadth and power to a body of work also filled with rich beauty and delight.

The Garden as a Place of Beauty

The art of the garden is an expression of beauty, an ordered realm that offers us pleasure and engages all of our senses. Indeed, a garden is the place where the garden designer works in partnership with the natural world, applying her sense of order and her knowledge of design principles to create a harmonious aesthetic. The successful gardener is a trained observer, attuned through all her sensory faculties, and must be attentive to her environment in order to refine and manipulate it. As both gardener and poet, Anne Spencer had a dual inclination to focus her observations. Her keen observations enrich her poetry immensely.

In "Life-Long, Poor Browning," the poet muses that her favorite

FIG. 32 *Anne Spencer in the living room of 1313 Pierce Street.*

FIG. 33 *The veranda of the Spencer house.*

FIG. 34 *The restored brick and turf driveway.*

FIG. 35 *Anne and Edward in the first garden room about 1941. Note the man in the background playing croquet in the garden of Warwick Spencer.*

FIG. 36 *The rear of the Spencer house, showing the two-story porch, now enclosed to form a first floor sunroom and second floor bedroom.*

FIG. 37 *The view of the restored garden from the second floor bedroom. Note the purple martin houses and Edankraal.*

FIG. 38 *The restored gate to the second garden room, originally constructed of recycled latticework from the former two-story porch.*

FIG. 39 *Edankraal, Anne Spencer's garden study.*

FIG. 40 *Interior of Edankraal. Anne's writing desk is oriented toward the long view of the garden. Note the cut-out figures of her grandchildren, the children of Chauncey and Anne, on the desk.*

FIG. 41 *The inscription above the door of Edankraal, including good luck horseshoe.*

poet never knew Virginia's natural beauties, or he would not have yearned for the pastoral landscape of England while spending his days surrounded by the formal geometry of Italian gardens during his residence in Italy. Spencer was familiar with various gardening traditions around the world. Here, however, she celebrates not garden artifice but the natural beauty of the spring landscape in her home state:

> Here canopied reaches of dogwood and hazel,
> Beech tree and redbud fine-laced in vines,
> Fleet clapping rills by lush fern and basil,
> Drain blue hills to lowlands scented with pines...[46]

The Emersonian theme of the pursuit of Beauty, whether expressed in the garden, the human figure, or other forms, recurs frequently in Spencer's work. In "Questing," she pleads outright:

> But let me learn now where Beauty is;
> I was born to know her mysteries,[47]

Earlier in the poem she states,

> My day is spent too far toward night
> To wander aimlessly and miss her place;
> To grope, eyes shut, and fingers touching space.

Age alone could not slow the poet's pursuit. The search for beauty was, for Anne Spencer, a life-long commitment. The garden especially was a place of rich reward in her quest.

The Garden as Sensual Delight

Anne Spencer's first published poem, "Before the Feast of Shushan," was a significant debut. She enchants her readers with a tale of a richly exotic Persian garden. The poem refers to a story told in the first chapter of the Book of Esther in the Hebrew Scriptures. At the feast King

Ahasuerus demands imperiously that his beautiful wife, Vashti, appear before him and his assembled friends. The queen refuses. In this powerfully romantic poem, Spencer imagines the conversation the king and queen might have had *before* the feast. She invokes the inspiration of all the senses—sight, sound, taste, touch, and smell. She speaks, too, to that something more, the sense of the magic of the place:

> Sorcerer, release the dreams born here when
> Drowsy, shifting palm-shade enspells the brain;[48]

The observations of the senses enrich the exotic and sensual qualities of the poem. The garden setting and botanical references ground the work and give it power. A simile of a pool struck to its depth by a moon-ray, an invocation of lips redder than a grape and petals to be forced wide, and other garden-inspired expressions lend a heady and seductive quality that captures the reader's attention and imagination.

In the introduction to *The Book of American Negro Poetry*, Johnson writes, "In her 'Before the Feast of Shushan,' she displays an opulence, the love of which has long been charged against the Negro as one of his naïve and childish traits, but which in art may infuse a much needed color, warmth and spirit of abandon into American poetry."[49] Anchored in scholarship and literary reference, yet rich with sensual energy, the poem gives evidence of an inspired and original creative sensibility. This same sensibility is visually apparent in archival images of Anne Spencer's garden. The garden incorporated lush profusion within a unifying structure. The poet was a creative soul embodying both discipline and passion.

The Garden as a Realm of Transformation

The theme of transformation occurs frequently in Anne Spencer's poetry and for her the garden is a logical place to investigate change. Any good gardener realizes that change is inevitable in the natural world. Change in her garden would unquestionably heighten the poet's awareness of change in life, change that is both affirming and painful.

"Requiem" discusses the natural processes of death, decay, and cyclical regeneration [fig. 58]. She writes,

> Oh, I who so wanted to own some earth,
> Am consumed by the earth instead:
> Blood into river
> Bone into land
>   The grave restores what finds its bed.
>
> Oh, I who did drink of Spring's fragrant clay,
> Give back its wine for other men:
> Breath into air
> Heart into grass
>   My heart bereft—I might rest then.[50]

Transformation is not simply from substance to substance. The poetic mind transforms the rich inspiration of the spring into a headier beverage to be shared with others. The bereft protagonist gains solace from the recognition that her body will return to the earth and provide sustenance for the beauty of future springs. This short poem contrasts expectation and reality, anguish and ease, life and death and rebirth.

A more literal transformation can be found in "Change," in which the speaker celebrates her reincarnation into a higher form, "such a splendid tree." The poem begins,

> This day is here I hoped would come at last,
> When I, a man, should live again a tree
> The dregs I drained with Life in days long passed
> Now thru my body courage in ecstasy[51]

This is not the voice of the gardener who sees herself as superior to her garden world. Nor is this evidence of a conventional Christian belief system that puts man in a position of dominion over the plants and animals. This is Anne Spencer the mystic, passionate in her conviction that such a metamorphosis would be to a higher existence, a more desirable state.

The Garden as Healer

In Anne Spencer's poetry and in her life, the garden is a place of restoration and healing. This is most evident in a poem that she wrote as a tribute to her best friend, James Weldon Johnson, after his untimely death in 1938. From their first meeting in 1918, which the poet described as "an act of God," Spencer found in Johnson a dear colleague, a highly refined individual, a creative spirit who cherished beauty as much as she [fig. 59]. Anne Spencer told her biographer, "Jim brought my life to vibrant being... He released my soul."[52] On occasion she referred to Johnson as "Gem." His death was a great loss to Spencer. Several poems may reflect her grief and despair. But in "For Jim, Easter Eve," the reader discovers what is the most powerful source of comfort for the poet:

> If ever a garden was a Gethsemane
> with old tombs set high against
> the crumpled olive tree—and lichen,
> this, my garden has been to me.
>
> ...
> What is sorrow but tenderness now
> in this earth-close frame of land and sky
> falling constantly into horizons
> of east and west, north and south;
> what is pain but happiness here
> amid these green and wordless patterns,—
> indefinite texture of blade and leaf:[53]

The biblical imagery is apt. In the Gospel accounts of the New Testament, Jesus retreats to the Garden of Gethsemane to pray. In the Gospel according to Matthew he says, "My soul is very sorrowful, even to death."[54] In this garden he finds solace and hope, and the courage to overcome suffering and accept his destiny. Anne Spencer's choice of this biblical image and its profound association is both sensitive and powerful. The garden provides comfort and restoration.

Anne Spencer's own garden must have been a source of comfort to her throughout her long life as she struggled with ill health, racial injustice, and numerous losses and disappointments. As a young woman she had read Emerson's words affirming Nature's power to restore. The act of gardening, working in close contact with nature, was therapeutic for Anne Spencer, and her garden was an oasis of solace and beauty for herself as well as for family and friends. [fig. 60]

The Garden as a Sacred Space

The poem "Substitution," one of Anne Spencer's favorite poems, presents an even more significant role for the garden. It is a place of philosophical insight and divine revelation. This poem reveals more strongly than any other the influence of Emerson on Spencer and suggests similarities to Emily Dickinson as well.[55] In a manner much like Emily Dickinson, Spencer begins her poem with a question,

> Is Life itself but many ways of thought,
> How real the tropic storm or lambent breeze
> Within the slightest convolution wrought
> Our mantled world and men-freighted seas?[56]

Spencer then explores the concept of God's thoughts as having created the world:

> God thinks...and being comes to ardent things:
> The splendor of the day-spent sun, love's birth,—

She continues with a specific example of the power of that thought and its unity with the human mind, which resembles a similar belief of Emerson:

> As here within this noisy peopled room
> My thought leans forward...quick! you're lifted clear

Of brick and frame to moonlit garden bloom,—
Absurdly easy, now, our walking, dear,
Talking, my leaning close to touch your face...
His All-Mind bids us keep this sacred place!

Such is the power of the poetic mind. The garden is a spiritual retreat, a world apart, to be held sacred by the garden visitor. It is the place in which to commune with the "All-Mind" of God that is imminent in nature and human consciousness. In other poems Spencer affirms that the garden can be a means of revelation of God. In "At the Carnival," the poet states, "Whatever is good is God." As we have seen, for her God is the source of all the earth's beauty and the world is an expression of the "All-Mind." She states this succinctly in an untitled poem that begins,

Thou art come to us, O God, this year—
Or how come these wisteria boughs
Dripping with the heavy honey of the Spring
Art here. For who but Thou could in living bring
This loveliness beyond all
Our words for prayer...[57]

Here, in the abundance of spring's glories [fig. 61], is proof of God's existence, she maintains. She goes on to reflect:

We thank Thee great God—
We who must now ever house
In the body-cramped places age has doomed—
That to us comes Even the sweet pangs
Of the Soul's illimitable sentience
Seeing the wisteria Thou has bloomed!

The ever-observant gardener, whose mind is now housed "in the body-cramped places age has doomed," goes beyond the powers of the five senses, through "the Soul's illimitable sentience." In a sequence of questions, then prayer and praise and celebration, the poet rejoices in the reality of God's existence revealed through the beauty of the garden.

A hitherto unpublished poem, "To John Keats, Poet, At Springtime," suggests a close connection to four of Spencer's garden poems[58] and serves to illustrate more clearly a number of these garden themes.[59] In four stanzas the poet speaks directly to Keats as her equal, an individual of refined sensibility with whom she shares a spiritual communion. Familiar themes abound. The poet rejoices in the world of nature as a place of beauty, a realm of transformation, and a revelation of the divine. Just as in "Change," where the poet becomes "a splendid tree," here her fellow poet is transformed into a maple tree, his fingers to grass:

> Somehow I feel your sensitive will
> Is pulsing up some tremulous
> Sap road of a maple tree, whose leaves
> Grow music as they grow, since your
> Wild voice is in them, a harp that grieves
> For life that opens death's dark door.
> Through dust, your fingers still can push
> The Vision Splendid to a birth,
> Though now they work as grass in the hush
> Of the night on the broad sweet page of the earth.[60]

As in "Requiem," where the poet's heart is transformed into grass, here Keats's fingers are at work in nature, nurturing its beauty. The last stanza offers an illuminating glimpse into Anne Spencer's sense of self. She contrasts what "they say" and what "I know":

> "John Keats is dead," they say, but I
> Who hear your full insistent cry
> In bud and blossom, leaf and tree,
> Know John Keats still writes poetry.
> And while my head is earthward bowed
> To read new life sprung from your shroud,
> Folks seeing me must think it strange
> That merely spring should so derange

My mind. They do not know that you,
John Keats, keep revel with me, too.

Anne Spencer is celebrating spring in the company of a rare kindred spirit, one who, like herself, is especially attuned to life's higher values. This recently discovered poem offers valuable insight into Anne Spencer, the poet, while enriching our understanding of the corpus of her work.

Critical to a deeper understanding of the poet and the influence of the garden on her creative sensibility is an appreciation of her need to revise and refine her work [figs. 62, 63, 64]. Anne Spencer's ongoing reworking of her poetry can be seen as a cultivation of her literary offspring, not dissimilar from the way she cultivated her children or herself, as well as her garden. At the age of ninety-five, Chauncey Spencer recalled the way his mother challenged her children to learn and improve their vocabularies and their intellects. He also related stories about his mother's high aesthetic standards, as evidenced by the ongoing changes in the design of the garden.[61] J. Lee Greene states that she was "concerned with perfection."[62] Fortunately, the very nature of the art of the garden invites repeated refinement. The living essence of the garden designer's palette ensures perpetual change, and the cyclical rhythms of the gardener's year make redesign possible and often necessary. Anne Spencer the gardener loved to experiment, to try out different effects in her garden. Similarly, Anne Spencer the poet could not resist the temptation to rework her crafted phrases and stanzas.

Ironically, Spencer's penchant to revise and refine may at times have rendered some of her thoughts a bit obscure. In his introduction to her poems in *The Book of American Negro Poetry*, James Weldon Johnson wrote, "At times her lines are so compact that they become almost cryptic, and have to be read more than once before they will yield their meaning and beauty."[63] Some of the forty-three poems underwent considerable revision. Other poems, in contrast, appear to be unfinished, works-in-progress not intended for an audience, seedlings still in the nursery. Anne Spencer wrote continually. She was engaged in an ongoing process, not consumed by the desire for a finished product. Such is the perspective of the true gardener.

FIG. 42 *The restored pergola, adjacent to Edankraal.*

FIG. 43 *The central section of the pergola, looking in the direction of the house.*

FIG. 44 *The statue of Minerva in the center of the restored pergola.*

FIG. 45 *The restored paths of the third garden room. In the 1930s this area was lushly planted with flowers.*

FIG. 46 *View of the fourth garden room, the pool garden, as framed through the grape arbor.*

FIG. 47 *The deutzia in bloom, arching over the curving concrete bench of the restored pool garden.*

FIG. 48 *The pool in the restored fourth room of the garden, looking back toward the grape arbor and Edankraal.*

FIG. 49 *The cast iron head of Prince Ebo, the gift of W.E.B. Du Bois.*

FIG. 50 *Anne Spencer at work in her garden, 1941.*

FIG. 51 *The Spencer's pet crow, Joe, poses for the camera next to an early version of the cottage garden fence. Anne Spencer loved birds and drew inspiration from the creatures in her garden.*

As a gardener Anne Spencer clearly extended certain philosophical observations from one creative realm to the other. In the world of nature, change is inevitable. Patience and persistence are necessary. Loyalty and optimism are rewarded. Humility is a lesson the garden teaches again and again. Just as Spencer's gardening enriched her poetry, her poetic wisdom deepened her relationship with her garden.

Anne Spencer composed her final poem in June of 1974, the year before she died at the age of ninety-three. Prophetically, perhaps, she entitled the poem "1975." In this last testament she deals with the power of the garden to nurture creativity.

> Turn an earth clod
> Peel a shaley rock
> In fondness molest a curly worm
> Whose *familiar* is everywhere
> Kneel
> And the curly worm   sentient *now*
> Will *light* the word that tells the poet what a poem is[64]

This poem can be seen as a distillation of her philosophy, an eloquently simple exposition on her sources of inspiration and processes of creation. The "soul's illimitable sentience"[65] is found now in the body of a humble worm which, by its daily acts of literally digesting the earth to enhance its fertility, presents a luminosity that offers the poet the very understanding of her craft. For how long had Spencer worked on this poem? It is a crystalline gem, the final creation of the poet whose work Jessie Fauset had praised fifty-two years earlier as having "a diamond clearness of exposition." A diamond drawn straight from the earth!

CHAPTER FIVE

THE GARDEN RESTORED

GARDENS ARE FRAGILE AND EPHEMERAL works of art. If they are not carefully maintained, they vanish or become a chaos of rampant weeds and deteriorating architectural fragments. Their serene order becomes disturbing disorder. Anne Spencer's garden had its own brush with oblivion. It was spared this fate through a carefully researched and labor-intensive garden restoration sustained by strong and committed leadership and dedicated volunteer labor.[66]

Anne Spencer's extremely high-maintenance garden began to decline in the last years of her life when loss of sight and other infirmities of old age prevented her from carrying out her demanding daily maintenance routine. In the eight-year period between her death in 1975 and the beginning of the restoration in 1983, the garden's decline accelerated. Rapidly growing honeysuckle, the bane of many a Virginia garden, smothered its flowers and shrubs. Poison ivy, the berries of which are so attractive to birds, climbed high in the trees. Ironically the fertile soil that Anne Spencer had enriched through seventy years of organic gardening practices nourished the fast-growing vines and weeds engulfing her garden. Its fountains fell silent and the pool filled with stagnant rainwater. The blue lattice gates were slowly rotting away. The pergola had vanished and only one post of the grape arbor remained. The tall purple martin houses suffered a similar fate. Edankraal was submerged in a forest of high weeds and vines like a sham ruin in an eighteenth-century English picturesque garden. The elegant cast iron border of the fence was heavily corroded, and its wire mesh full of holes. Traces of the garden's former self continued to exist—the layout of the path system, many of the trees, and Edankraal, although the latter was in great need of repair. Anne's ailing garden clearly required radical surgery if it was to survive, and fortunately that surgery was forthcoming.

Our first venture into Anne's garden called upon our imaginations to visualize it in its late 1930s form [fig. 20]. What visitors now experience at the beginning of the twenty-first century is a painstakingly restored garden based on that same time period.

The garden's restoration effort revolved in large part around the intelligence, vision, energy, and dedication of a single individual. Jane Baber White [fig. 65], a local professional garden designer acting as a volunteer, thoroughly researched the garden, developed a feasible plan for its restoration [fig. 66], recruited volunteers, and raised funds. Yet garden restoration is complex. Gardens by their very nature can never be static entities. The alchemy of a garden over time is the result of a subtle blend of nature's processes and the garden designer's ever-changing visions of new possibilities. In addition, adapting a private garden for public visitation and maintaining it on a limited budget with a small force of volunteer labor inevitably necessitates some changes. For Jane White a key issue was what specific period of the garden's long life would guide the restoration. After carefully researching all phases of the garden, Jane White chose its late 1930s form [fig. 20]. Her choice was a wise one for many reasons. The more abundant floral displays of the garden's earlier form, which Jane White knew quite well and admired, are indeed striking [fig. 18], but features of the late 1930s, such as the graceful grape arbor and subtle spatial expression in the fourth garden room, represent a more sophisticated and mature state of the garden's design. Also, numerous Spencer family photographs document this period of the garden, making an informed restoration effort possible. An important additional advantage of this phase is its lower maintenance. As we have seen in chapter two, by this time Anne Spencer had replaced the abundant herbaceous planting of the fourth garden room [fig. 19] with turf and a few ornamental trees [fig. 20].

A consortium of civic-minded individuals and organizations, including the Hillside Garden Club, high school students, Boy Scouts, local contractors [fig. 67], and members of the Spencer family meshed their labor and resources for the restoration effort. The deteriorated gravel walkways were repaired and edged with brick to accommodate heavy visitation. Jane White replaced higher maintenance privet hedges with English boxwood, which require less pruning. The present pergola is a simplified version of the original, which was supported by diagonal bracing and vertical turned wooden posts echoing those of the Edankraal porch [figs. 14, 42]. These were simply too expensive to replicate. Roses originally distributed throughout the garden were grouped as a single rose garden for ease of maintenance, forming an anteroom before the main lattice gate. Jane White planted an evergreen screen along the border of the rose garden to buffer it from the adjacent lot, which was no longer owned by Spencer relatives. The most visible change is simplification of the earlier high-maintenance planting plan. An extensive central area of the third garden room framed by the pergola and grape arbor was once lushly planted with a jewel-like abundance of flowers and heavily-textured leafy ornamentals. These have been replaced with lower-maintenance lawn [fig. 45]. The intensive daily care this area required in its earlier form is an eloquent testimony to Anne Spencer's deep commitment to her garden. These necessary changes notwithstanding, the restored garden we visit today retains the sophisticated scale and spatial organization of the late 1930s garden, provides many of the sensual delights of its planting plan, and maintains the original elegance of its details, many of which have been carefully restored to their former quality.

In the spring of 1983, Chauncey Spencer, Anne Spencer's son, initiated the restoration by seeking assistance from Jane White and he substantially aided the research with his memories and collection of garden photographs. The garden's restoration began in the fall of 1983. The work was greatly assisted by volunteers from the Hillside Garden Club, a local chapter of the Garden Club of Virginia.

The restoration effort was meticulous and energetic. At great expense, three hundred feet of the original cast iron trim on the top of the bordering fence was removed in one-foot segments, carefully cleaned and stored [fig. 68]. It was later reinstalled. Hillside Garden Club volunteers carefully dug up all surviving flowers and bulbs and planted them in holding beds in Jane White's vegetable garden and the gardens of other members while the site was being cleared of weeds. Like dedicated archeologists, on hands and knees, with trowels and boxes in hand, they sifted the earth seeking the smallest bulbs, working rapidly in front of the excavating equipment that was clearing the site for restoration. So overgrown was the garden that volunteers had to remove twenty-five dump truck loads of debris [fig. 69]. Chauncey Spencer commissioned the rebuilding of the purple martin houses and reinstalled them on their twenty-one foot poles with the help of a local contractor, utilizing an elaborate thirty-foot-high scaffolding and pulley system. Boy Scout Troop 19, spearheaded by Stuart Desso, Jr., rebuilt the pergola [fig. 70] and grape arbor, and a team of local high school students received extra credit for laying the brick borders of the paths during their spring vacation. The fountains and underground pipe system were put into working order and Prince Ebo once more spouted into the quiet pool which was replanted with waterlilies [fig. 71]. The statue of Minerva was replaced in its former position in the center of the pergola, although it has since been removed because of its deteriorating condition.

The first year's labor primed and stretched the garden's canvas and restored its architectural bones, readying it for replanting. This was begun in the spring of 1984. The garden club members focused their initial efforts on the first garden room next to the rear of the house [fig. 73]. Their volunteers' archeology had yielded thirty-five gnarled and overgrown original rose plants. Jane White recalls their amazing, contorted configurations. They were replanted and all survived. Carl Cato, a distinguished local heritage rose expert, identified such varieties as Climbing Crimson Glory, Climbing American Beauty, Blaze, Betty Prior, American Pillar, Aloha, Mother's Day, and Mme Grégoire Staechelin. To simplify maintenance, all the roses were concentrated in the present-day "rose garden." What we view today are all original plants, which continue to thrive with careful tending by Anne Spencer House and Garden Museum volunteers and the assistance of a professional rosarian.

The replanting of the remaining areas of the garden soon followed [fig. 74]. Some original snowdrops and narcissus had survived and were replanted along the flagstone walk opposite the roses. Additional bulbs were donated by the Sweet Briar College Alumnae Association [fig. 75].

Several springs after the restoration, thousands of ipheion, a pale blue diminutive bulb that Anne had originally planted in the garden, appeared, "as if by magic," under the dogwood in the first garden room. It was as if, said Jane White, the garden was affirming the restoration. The two narrow borders that frame the garden on its east and west boundaries were replanted with different palettes influenced by old photographs from the late 1930s and additional discoveries during the clearing of the site. The west border was planted with purple and white lilac to form a hedge and was underplanted with periwinkle and bulbs. The east border was rendered as a kaleidoscope of colorful perennials and annuals that were also present in the archival photographs: poppies, peonies, irises, daylilies [fig. 76], foxgloves, hollyhocks, daisies, phlox, chrysanthemums, coral bells, hostas, candy tuft, petunias, nasturtiums, sweet peas, and snapdragons. Hillside Garden Club members donated plants from their own gardens to assist this effort. Such a lush, sparkling array of bloom had at one time created a carpet of color that covered the entire ground plane of the third garden room from the grape arbor to the Edankraal pergola. Today this high-maintenance, multicolored tapestry has been replaced by serene mown lawn panels. As we gaze at the narrow strip of color along the restored east border, we need but unroll it in our imaginations across the entire third garden room to realize the celebration of color and texture that was an important feature of the late 1930s garden. Also, the third room's grape arbor was replanted with Concord and Niagara grapes, an educated guess at the time that was later verified by the discovery of a poem by Anne Spencer featuring these two varieties.[67] Finally, given the fact that gardens are dynamic ecosystems, the growth of surviving hardwoods has created a denser shade canopy and some of the columnar Virginia cedars originally framing the pool in the fourth garden room have died and been removed.

Such an impressive restoration effort has been achieved on a very modest budget. Between 1983 and 1984, $8000 and many hours of volunteer labor painstakingly revived much of Anne Spencer's sophisticated work of garden art. An additional $6000 provided by the Garden Club of Virginia's prestigious "Common Wealth Award" for 1985 not only recognized the quality of the restoration but enabled reconstruction of the main garden gate, lattice fence, and brick pavers in its adjacent driveway [figs. 72, 34]. Jane White continued to be active in the restoration effort for eight years on a daily basis after the initial work was completed in 1985. Today the garden is preserved and maintained by the Anne Spencer House and Garden Museum, Inc. Jane White now focuses her efforts on the preservation of yet another of Lynchburg's important cultural landscapes, the Old City Cemetery, only one mile away.

The Anne Spencer home and garden remains an important cultural resource for the city of Lynchburg and the surrounding region. The site has been designated a Virginia Historic Landmark, a Friends of the Library USA Literary Landmark, a Historic Landmark by the Association for the Study for Afro-American Life and History in association with the Amoco Foundation, Inc., and is included in the National Register of Historic Places. After his retirement from a distinguished career in aviation, civil rights, and public administration, Chauncey Spencer hosted informative tours of the house and the restored garden until his death on August 21, 2002 [figs. 77, 78]. Today the Anne Spencer House and Garden Museum, Inc. supervises field trips for local elementary, junior high and high school, and college students, and sponsors seminars dealing with African-American history and culture. Thus it has gone beyond the more traditional role of a house museum and restored garden to preserve an intellectual legacy derived from the tradition of spirited, far-ranging conversation that once resonated in the parlor and garden rooms of 1313 Pierce Street when Anne and Edward were hosts to leaders of the Harlem Renaissance.

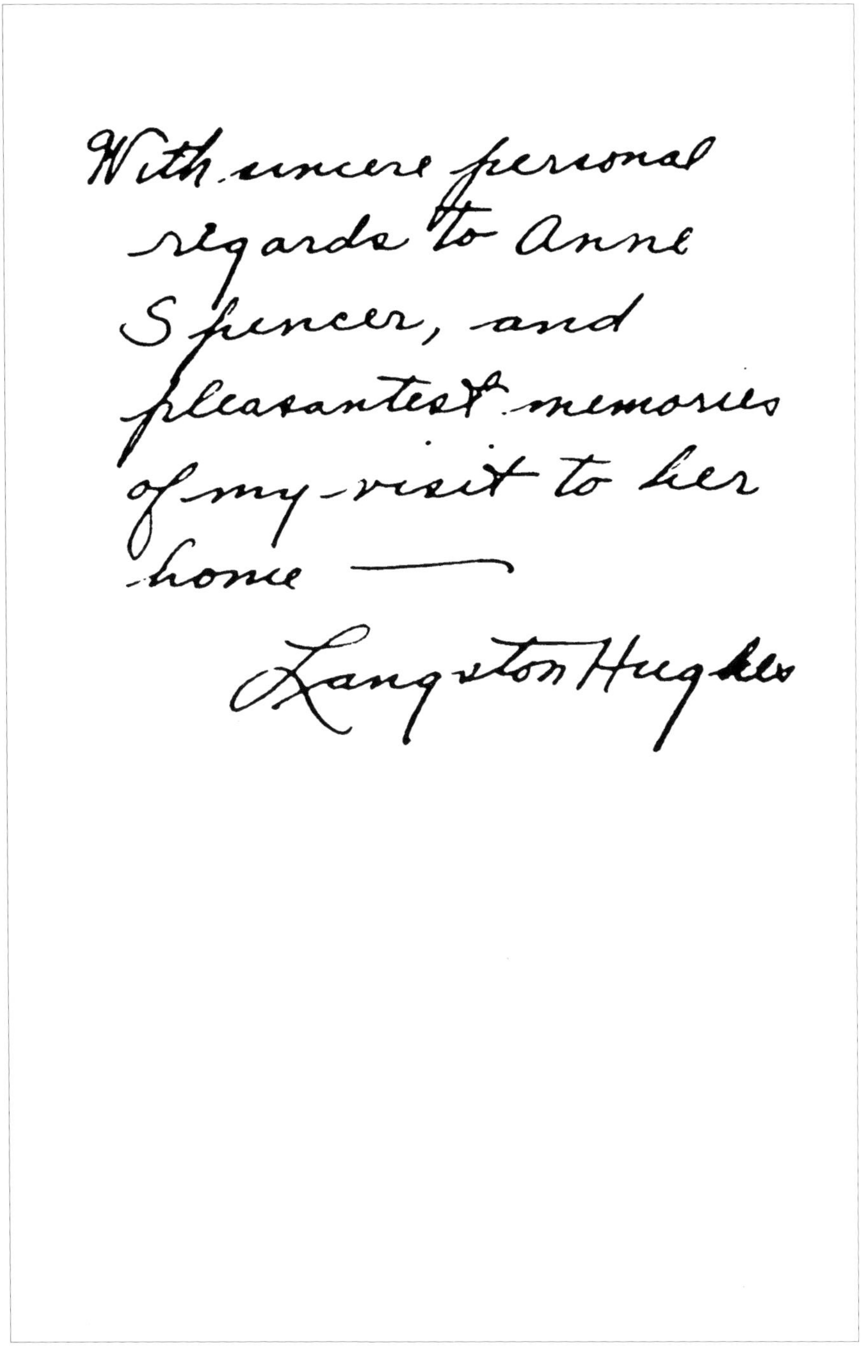

With sincere personal
regards to Anne
Spencer, and
pleasantest memories
of my visit to her
home —

Langston Hughes

FIG. 52 *Thank you note from Langston Hughes, a close friend of Anne Spencer.*

FIG. 53 *Chauncey and his wife, Anne Howard Spencer, during a summer visit to the garden in the 1940s.*

FIG. 54 *Anne and Edward in the garden with two of their ten grandchildren.*

FIG. 55 *Anne Spencer seated at a writing desk, reflected in an ornate mirror in the living room.*

FIG. 56 *Anne Spencer's favorite flower, the nasturtium.*

FIG. 57 *Grapes thrive on the restored pergola.*

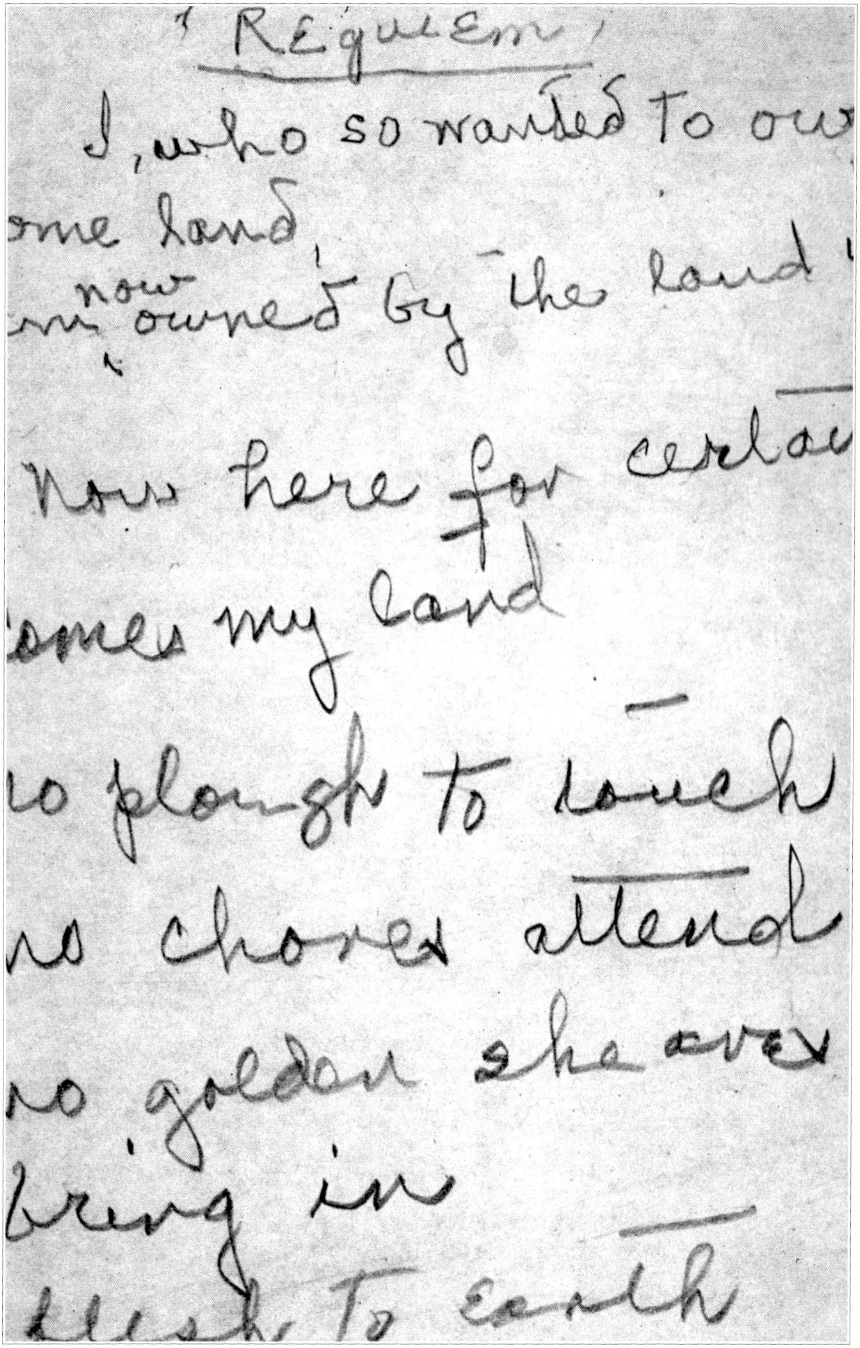

"Requiem"

I, who so wanted to ow
ome land,
now
m owned by the land
Now here for certai
omes my land
o plough to touch
o chores attend
o golden sheaves
bring in
flesh to earth

FIG. 58 *An earlier draft of Anne Spencer's poem "Requiem" showing revisions. Note the contrast with the version on page 133 published in* LYRIC, *Spring 1931.*

FIG. 59 *Anne Spencer's inscribed photograph of James Weldon Johnson, "To Anne Bethel Spencer, herself a true poet, with the sincere regards of James Weldon Johnson, April 14, 1921."*

FIG. 60 *Delicate pink phlox in the restored garden contribute to its beauty and tranquility.*

CHAPTER SIX

THE GENIUS OF THE PLACE

ANNE SPENCER'S GARDEN, THE STORIES ABOUT the life she lived there, and the poems she wrote there, all offer insight into each other, and collectively they give us rich clues about the mind and soul of this rare, creative individual. The poetry and her garden clearly spring from the same deep wellspring of creativity. Anne Spencer cultivated all that she touched diligently, ceaselessly. She brought to all her creative endeavors—in poetry and garden design, political action and education—a discipline, a commitment to preparation, and a questing need to work and rework, refining tirelessly all to which she set her mind. She did her work with great passion and the full engagement of all her senses.

Anne Spencer was a complex individual, both very public and intensely private. She was known in her community as an outspoken advocate for justice and a fervent proponent of equal opportunity and quality education for all. As a political activist she worked energetically to advance the rights of African-Americans in Lynchburg. As a librarian and educator she spent her days in the nurture and cultivation of young students to prepare them for a better future. While Anne Spencer was very visible in Lynchburg, her reputation extended to a far wider world, primarily because of her creative accomplishments as a published poet and her legendary hospitality. Admired for her impeccably high standards in all aspects of her life, she was recognized for her outspoken, defiant spirit and her fierce sense of independence.

Privately, on the other hand, Anne Spencer was an introverted individual who required long periods of solitude to restore her depleted spirit. In her biographical note in Countee Cullen's *Caroling Dusk*, an anthology of poetry published in 1927, Anne Spencer wrote:

> Mother Nature, February, forty five years ago forced me on the stage that I, in turn, might assume the role of lonely child, happy wife, per-

> plexed mother—and so far, a twice resentful grandmother. I have no academic honors, nor lodge regalia. I am a Christian by intention, a Methodist by inheritance, and a Baptist by marriage.... I proudly love being a Negro woman—its (sic) so involved and interesting. *We* are the PROBLEM—the great national game of TABOO.[68]

She used her garden as a restorative sanctuary to which she could retreat in fatigue, frustration, or sorrow, as well as in celebration. Safe within its boundaries Anne Spencer exercised her creative energies, designing the garden rooms and her ever-changing plant palette and creating her poetry [fig. 79]. There was a rich cross-fertilization between her poems and the artistic expression of her garden. Throughout her long life Anne Spencer nurtured and cultivated her own creative soul as well as her work, her home and her garden, her family and friends, her students and her acquaintances. She was a perfectionist.

Many visitors to Anne Spencer's house and garden have remarked upon the power of the place. To be alone in the garden, savoring the rich sensory stimulation, is a gift. Some two centuries before Anne Spencer, another poet, Alexander Pope, exhorted the would-be designer of gardens to "Consult the genius of the place in all."[69] What is the genius of Anne's garden, this rare private world of the poet? More than twenty-five years after her death the garden still holds a magic, a genius, that is palpable. Especially at dusk an enchantment falls over the place. Birds sing all day long, but by evening their song suggests they have taken full possession of this tranquil garden as their own. It is a quiet beauty of long shadows, the gentle touch of an evening breeze, the allure of rich fragrances. Its alchemy dissolves cares and quickens the imagination. The genius of the place endures, an invitation to all who would visit and take the time to sit, to feel the inspiration it offers. As noted on the nomination form of the National Register of Historic Places, "Few of the nation's literary shrines so effectively invoke the presence of their former occupant."[70] One explanation for this power of place might be found in the unity of Anne Spencer's creative work and her innermost being. Her short poem entitled "He Said" expresses this best:

> Your garden at dusk
> Is the soul of love
> Blurred in its beauty
> And softly caressing;
> I, gently daring,
> This sweetest confessing,
> Say your garden at dusk
> Is your soul, My love.[71]

As Anne's son, Chauncey, so aptly described her gardening journey, "Her garden was her life. That garden *is* my mother."[72]

A SELECTION OF POETRY

THE POETRY OF ANNE SPENCER IS RICH and highly personal with many layers of meaning. The seventeen poems that follow are filled with images, symbols, metaphors and similes that center on the garden. Just as a well-designed garden invites deeper exploration and reveals its beauty as we wander its paths, these poems reward us with understanding and insight as we spend more time with them. Their idiosyncratic vocabulary and unconventional syntax often surprise, confound and delight. Their complexities and nuances prove them worthy of ongoing investigation. Anne Spencer wrote continually throughout her long life and addressed a wide variety of ideas complementing her garden themes. However, these seventeen poems centered on the garden read well as a group and collectively they offer us a glimpse inside the garden's boundaries to the very heart of the poet. The poems appear in the order they are discussed in the text.[73]

ANY WIFE TO ANY HUSBAND:
A Derived Poem

This small garden is half my world
I am nothing to it—when all is said,
I plant the thorn and kiss the rose,
But they will grow when I am dead.

Let not this change, Love, the human life
Share with her the joy you had with me,
List with her the plaintive bird you heard with me.
Feel all human joys, but
Feel most a "shadowy third."

[EARTH, I THANK YOU}

Earth, I thank you
for the pleasure of your language
You've had a hard time
bringing it to me
from the ground
to grunt thru the noun
To all the way
feeling   seeing   smelling   touching
—awareness
I am here!

Lines to a Nasturtium
(A Lover Muses)

Flame-flower, Day-torch, Mauna Loa,
I saw a daring bee, today, pause, and soar,
  Into your flaming heart;
Then did I hear crisp, crinkled laughter
As the furies after tore him apart?
  A bird, next, small and humming,
Looked into your started depths and fled...
Surely, some dread sight, and dafter
  Than human eyes as mine can see,
Set the stricken air waves drumming
  In his flight.

Day-torch, Flame-flower, cool-hot Beauty,
I cannot see, I cannot hear your flutey
Voice lure your loving swain,
But I know one other to whom you are in beauty
Born in vain:
Hair like the setting sun,
Her eyes a rising star,
Motions gracious as reeds by Babylon, bar
All your competing;
Hands like, how like, brown lilies sweet,
Cloth of gold were fair enough to touch her feet...
Ah, how the sense reels at my repeating,
As once in her fire-lit heart I felt the furies
Beating, beating.[74]

Grapes: Still-Life

Snugly you rest, sweet globes,
Aged essence of the sun;
Copper of the platter
Like that you lie upon.

Is so well your heritage
You need feel no change
From the ringlet of your stem
To this bright rim's flange;

You green-white Niagara,
Cool dull Nordic of your kind,—
Does your thick meat flinch
From these...touch and press your rind?

Caco, there, so close to you,
Is the beauty of the vine;
Stamen red and pistil black
Thru the curving line;

Concord, the too peaceful one
Purpling at your side,
All the colors of his flask
Holding high in pride...

This, too, is your heritage,
You who force the plight;
Blood and bone you turn to them
For their root is white.[75]

FIG. 61 *Spring blooms in the restored rose garden – larkspur mixes with roses. The beauty of nature was a revelation of God for Anne Spencer.*

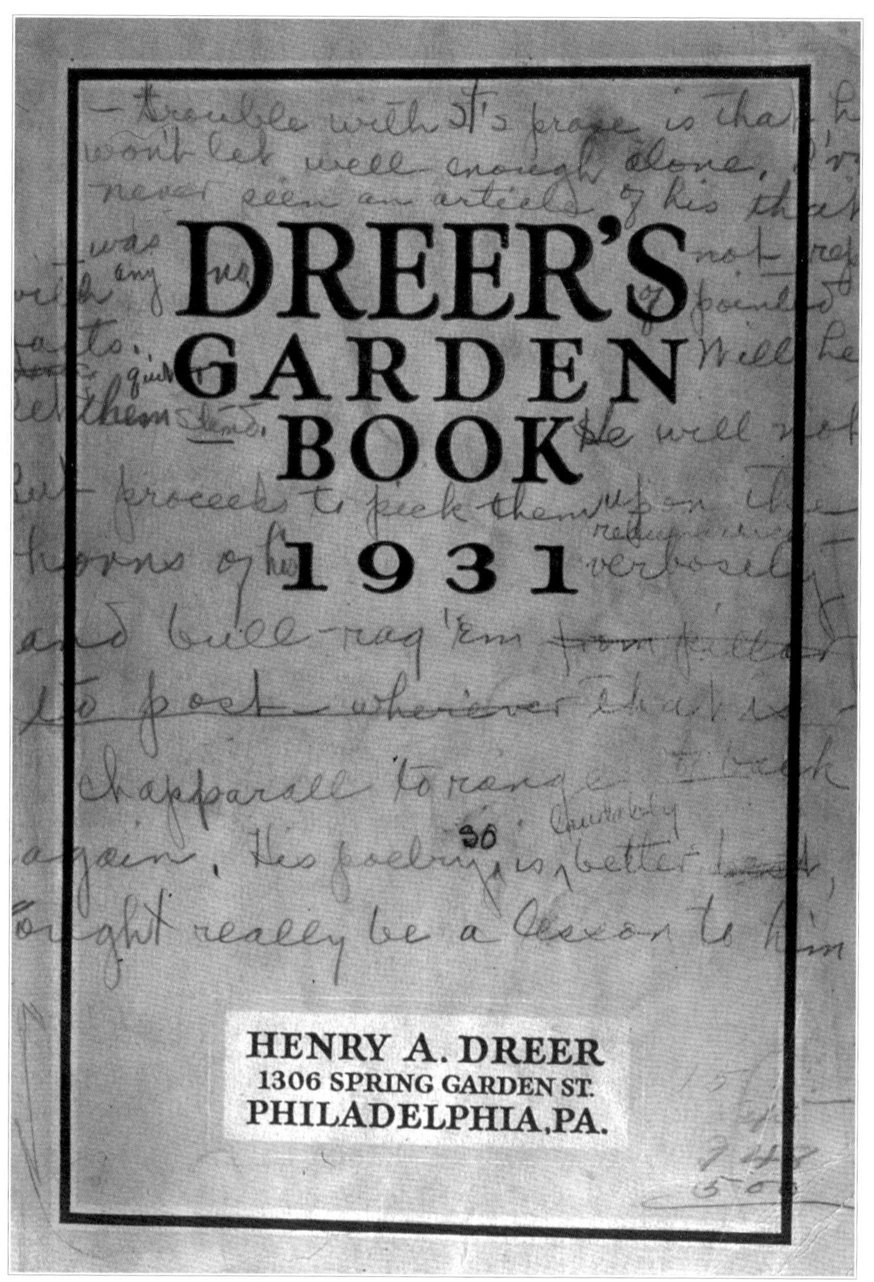

FIG. 62 *Anne Spencer wrote on whatever materials were at hand. In this example, she critiques the prose style of an unidentified author on the cover of a nursery catalog.*

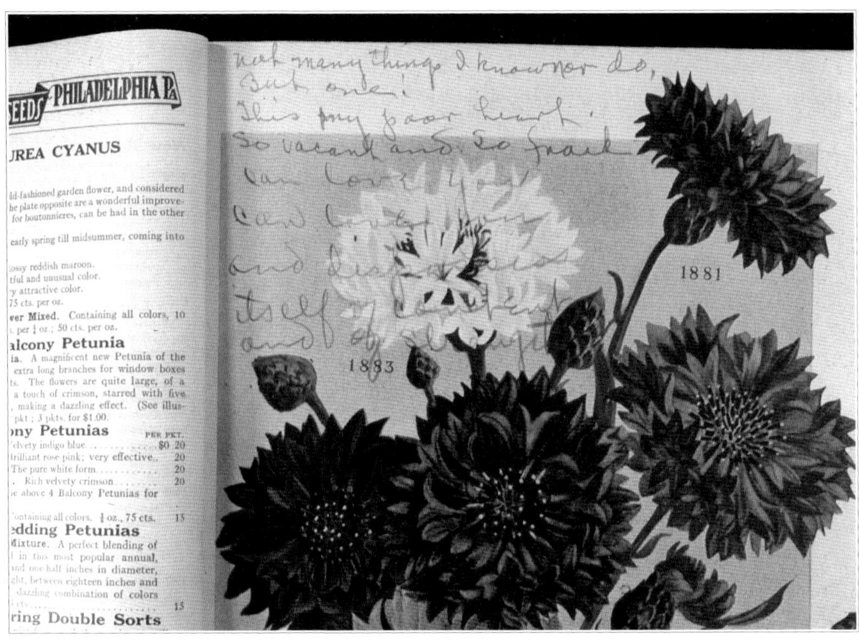

FIG. 63 *One of Anne Spencer's unpublished poems, written on a page of* DREER'S GARDEN BOOK *of 1931.*

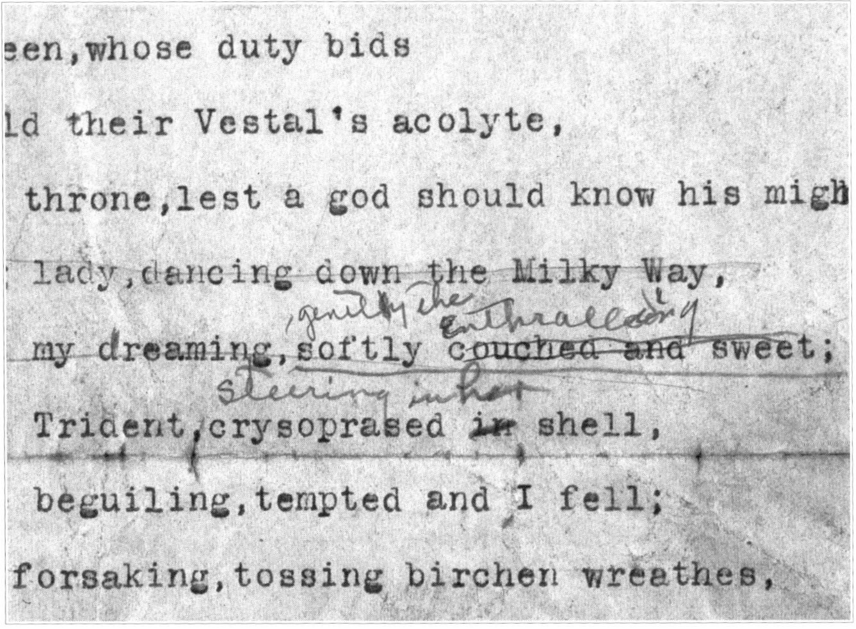

een, whose duty bids
ld their Vestal's acolyte,
throne, lest a god should know his migh
lady, dancing down the Milky Way,
my dreaming, softly ~~couched and~~ gently the enthralling sweet;
Trident, steering in her crysoprased ~~in~~ shell,
beguiling, tempted and I fell;
forsaking, tossing birchen wreathes,

FIG. 64 *After many revisions, Anne Spencer had her poems typed. She continued to revise her typed manuscripts.*

FIG. 65 *Jane Baber White speaking in the garden on the occasion of a lecture by J. Lee Greene, Anne Spencer's biographer.*

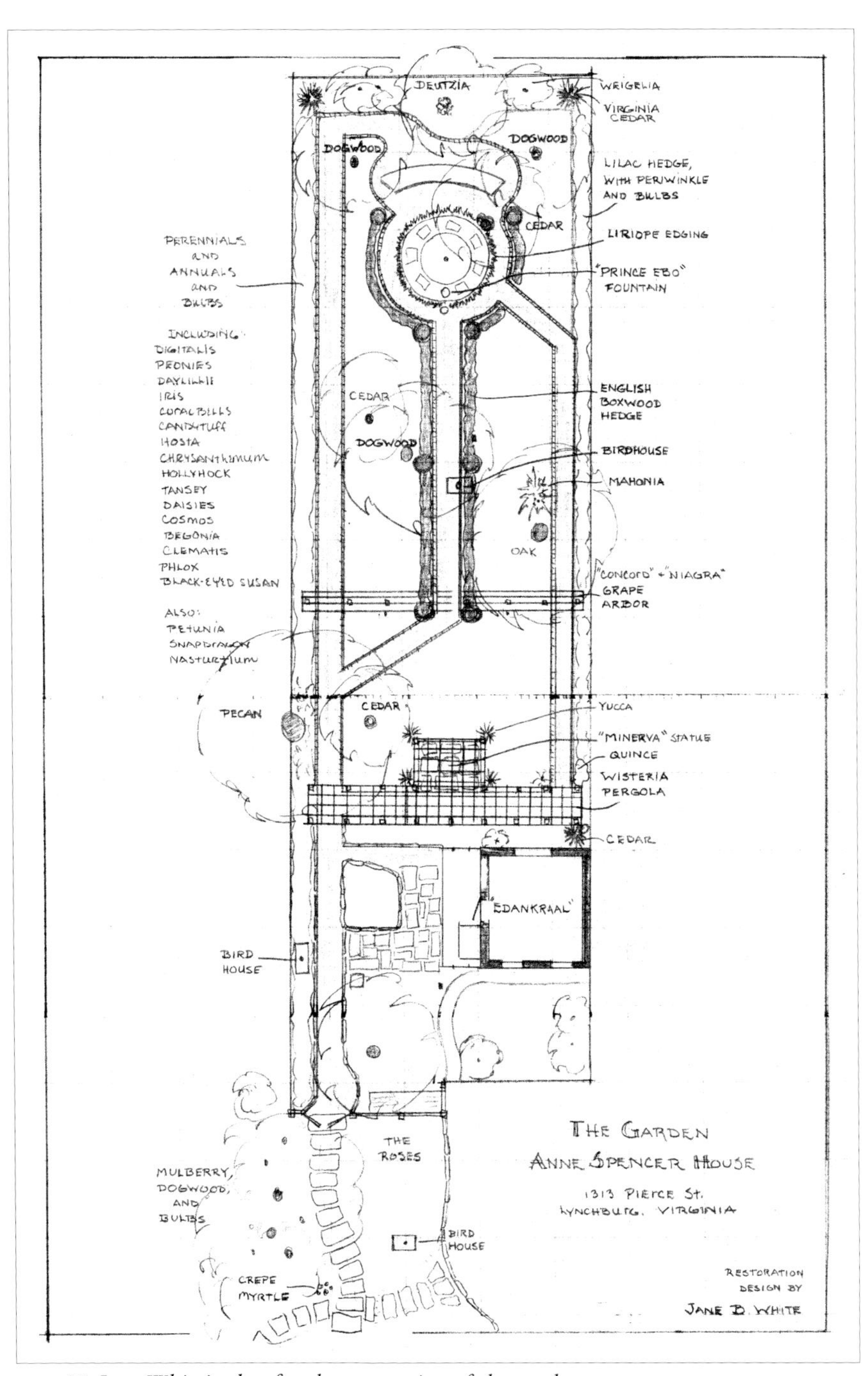

FIG. 66 *Jane White's plan for the restoration of the garden.*

FIG. 67 *Local contractor, Addison Wood, and his son, Ladd, were hired to rebuild the lattice fence.*

FIG. 68 *Application of the cast iron trim to the refurbished garden fence.*

FIG. 69 *One of the twenty-five truckloads of debris removed from the garden.*

Creed

If my garden oak spares one bare ledge
For boughed mistletoe to grow and wedge;
And all the wild birds this year should know
I cherish their freedom to come and go;
If a battered worthless dog, masterless, alone,
Slinks to my heels, sure of bed and bone;
And the boy just moved in, deigns a glance-assay,
Turns his pockets inside out, calls, "Come and play!"
If I should surprise in the eyes of my friend
That the deed was *my* favor he'd let me lend;
Or hear it repeated from a foe I despise,
That I whom he hated was chary of lies;
If a pilgrim stranger, fainting and poor,
Followed an urge and rapped at my door,
And my husband loves me till death puts apart,
Less as flesh unto flesh, more as heart unto heart:
I may challenge God when we meet That Day,
And He dare not be silent or send me away.[76]

[GOD NEVER PLANTED A GARDEN]

God never planted a garden
But He placed a keeper there;
And the keeper ever razed the ground
And built a city where
God cannot walk at the eve of day,
Nor take the morning air.

Life-Long, Poor Browning

Life-long, poor Browning never knew Virginia,
Or he'd not grieved in Florence for April sallies
Back to English gardens after Euclid's linear;
Clipt yews, Pomander Walks, and pleachéd alleys;

Primroses, prim indeed, in quite ordered hedges,
Waterways, soberly, sedately enchanneled,
No thin riotous blade even among among the sedges,
All the wild country-side tamely impaneled...

Dead, now, dear Browning lives on in heaven,—
(Heaven's Virginia when the year's at its Spring)
He's haunting the byways of wine-aired leaven
And throating the notes of the wildings on wing:

Here canopied reaches of dogwood and hazel,
Beech tree and redbud fine-laced in vines,
Fleet clapping rills by lush fern and basil,
Drain blue hills to lowlands scented with pines...

Think you he meets in this tender green sweetness
Shade that was Elizabeth...immortal completeness![77]

Questing

Let me learn now where Beauty is;
My day is spent too far toward night
To wander aimlessly and miss her place;
To grope, eyes shut, and fingers touching space.

Her maidens I have known, seen durance beside,
Handmaidens to the Queen, whose duty bids
Them lie and lure afield their Vestal's acolyte,
Lest a human shake the throne, lest a god should know his might:
Nereid, daughter of the Trident, steering in her shell,
Paused in voyage, smile beguiling, tempted and I fell;
Spiteful dryads, sport forsaking, tossing birchen wreathes,
Left the Druidic priests they teased so
In the oaken trees, crying, "Ho a mortal! here a believer!"
Bound me, she who held the sceptre, stricken by her, ah, deceiver...
But let me learn now where Beauty is;
I was born to know her mysteries,
And needing wisdom I must go in vain:
Being sworn bring to some hither land,
Leaf from her brow, light from her torchéd hand.[78]

Before the Feast of Shushan

Garden of Shushan!
After Eden, all terrace, pool, and flower recollect thee:
Ye weavers in saffron and haze and Tyrian purple,
Tell yet what range in color wakes the eye;
Sorcerer, release the dreams born here when
Drowsy, shifting palm-shade enspells the brain;
And sound! ye with harp and flute ne'er essay
Before these star-noted birds escaped from paradise awhile to
Stir all dark, and dear, and passionate desire, till mine
Arms go out to be mocked by the softly kissing body of the wind —
Slave, send Vashti to her King!

The fiery wattles of the sun startle into flame
The marbled towers of Shushan:
So at each day's wane, two peers—the one in
Heaven, the other on earth—welcome with their
Splendor the peerless beauty of the Queen.

Cushioned at the Queen's feet and upon her knee
Finding glory for mine head,—still, nearly shamed
Am I, the King, to bend and kiss with sharp
Breath the olive-pink of sandaled toes between;
Or lift me high to the magnet of a gaze, dusky,
Like the pool when but the moon-ray strikes to its depth;
Or closer press to crush a grape 'gainst lips redder
Than the grape, a rose in the night of her hair;
Then—Sharon's Rose in my arms.

And I am hard to force the petals wide;
And you are fast to suffer and be sad.
Is any prophet come to teach a new thing
Now in a more apt time?
Have him 'maze how you say love is sacrament;

How says Vashti, love is both bread and wine;
How to the altar may not come to break and drink;
Hulky flesh nor fleshly spirit!

I, thy lord, like not manna for meat as a Judahn;
I, thy master, drink, and red wine, plenty, and when
I thirst. Eat meat, and full, when I hunger.
I, thy King, teach you and leave you, when I list.
No woman in all Persia sets out strange action
To confuse Persia's lord—
Love is but desire and thy purpose fulfillment;
I, thy King, so say![79]

Requiem

Oh, I who so wanted to own some earth,
Am consumed by the earth instead:
Blood into river
Bone into land
The grave restores what finds its bed.

Oh, I who did drink of Spring's fragrant clay,
Give back its wine for other men:
Breath into air
Heart into grass
My heart bereft—I might rest then.[80]

Change

This day is here I hoped would come at last,
When I, a man, should live again a tree
The dregs I drained with Life in days long passed
Now thru my body courage in ecstasy
Awhile I lived apprenticed warm to flesh
And son the passioned errands of the sun:
Where lifted on the wing of some bright mesh
Of streaming wind, or dropped too deep, and spun
Into some dark abyss of circling wave,—
If so a votary come to Charybdis
With his clear torch fed from a heart—and as brave
Still now that I am such a splendid tree
There is only God and man to buffet me.
Can only those who hate you, Life, know bliss...

FIG. 70 *The pergola and Edankraal during reconstruction by the Boy Scouts..*

FIG. 71 *Waterlily in the restored pool.*

FIG. 72 *The brick and turf driveway under reconstruction.*

FIG. 73 *Stepping stone path in the restored first garden room. Aegopodium or Bishop's Weed blooms profusely in the spring.*

FIG. 74 *Volunteers from the Hillside Garden Club planting boxwood along the center path of the Pool Garden.*

FIG. 75 *Garden club volunteers planting bulbs in the square bed in front of Edankraal.*

FIG. 76 *A daylily in the east border of the restored garden.*

FIG. 77 *Chauncey Spencer in 1937. His pioneering flight from Chicago to Washington, D.C., led to the inclusion of African-American pilots in the military.*

FIG. 78 *Chauncey Spencer before the front door of the Spencer house preparing to lead a tour.*

FIG. 79 *Anne Spencer photographed in 1927, surrounded by the lush restorative beauty of her garden.*

For Jim, Easter Eve

If ever a garden was a Gethsemane,
with old tombs set high against
the crumpled olive tree—and lichen,
this, my garden has been to me.
For such as I none other is so sweet:
Lacking old tombs, here stands my grief,
and certainly its ancient tree.

Peace is here and in every season
a quiet beauty.
The sky falling about me
evenly to the compass...
What is sorrow but tenderness now
in this earth-close frame of land and sky
falling constantly into horizons
of east and west, north and south;
what is pain but happiness here
amid these green and wordless patterns,—
indefinite texture of blade and leaf:

Beauty of an old, old tree,
last comfort in Gethsemane.[81]

Substitution

Is Life itself but many ways of thought,
How real the tropic storm or lambent breeze
Within the slightest convolution wrought
Our mantled world and men-freighted seas?
God thinks . . . and being comes to ardent things:
The splendor of the day-spent sun, love's birth, —
Or dreams a little, while creation swings
The circle of His mind and Time's full girth . . .
As here within this noisy peopled room
My thought leans forward . . . quick! you're lifted clear
Of brick and frame to moonlit garden bloom, —
Absurdly easy, now, our walking, dear,
Talking, my leaning close to touch your face . . .
His All-Mind bids us keep this sacred place![82]

[Thou art come to us, O God, this year]

Thou art come to us, O God, this year—
Or how come these wisteria boughs
Dripping with the heavy honey of the Spring
Art here. For who but Thou could in living bring
This loveliness beyond all
Our words for prayer
And blur of leafish shadows, leaf in ochre,
Orchid of bloom with bright tears
Of Thy April's grief
We thank Thee great God—
We who must now ever house
In the body-cramped places age has doomed—
That to us come Even the sweet pangs
Of the Soul's illimitable sentience
Seeing the wisteria Thou has bloomed!

To John Keats, poet, at Springtime

I cannot hold my peace, John Keats;
There never was a spring like this;
It is an echo, that repeats
My last year's song and next year's bliss.
I know, in spite of all men say
Of Beauty, you have felt her most.
Yea, even in your grave her way
Is laid. Poor, troubled, lyric ghost,
Spring never was so fair and dear
As Beauty makes her seem this year.

I cannot hold my peace, John Keats;
I am as helpless in the toil
Of Spring as any lamb that bleats
To feel the solid earth recoil
Beneath his puny legs. Spring beats
Her tocsin call to those who love her,
And lo! the dogwood petals cover
Her breast with drifts of snow, and sleek
White gulls fly screaming to her, and hover
About her shoulders, and kiss her cheek,
While white and purple lilacs muster
Of color and odor; for her sake
All things that slept are now awake.

And you and I, shall we lie still,
John Keats, while Beauty summons us?
Somehow I feel your sensitive will
Is pulsing up some tremulous
Sap road of a maple tree, whose leaves
Grow music as they grow, since your
Wild voice is in them, a harp that grieves

For life that opens death's dark door.
Through dust, your fingers still can push
The Vision Splendid to a birth,
Though now they work as grass in the hush
Of the night on the broad sweet page of the earth.

"John Keats is dead," they say, but I
Who hear your full insistent cry
In bud and blossom, leaf and tree,
Know John Keats still writes poetry.
And while my head is earthward bowed
To read new life sprung from your shroud,
Folks seeing me must think it strange
That merely spring should so derange
My mind. They do not know that you,
John Keats, keep revel with me, too.

1975

Turn an earth clod
Peel a shaley rock
In fondness molest a curly worm
Whose *familiar* is everywhere
Kneel
And the curly worm   sentient *now*
Will *light* the word that tells the poet what a poem is

He Said:

"Your garden at dusk
Is the soul of love
Blurred in its beauty
And softly caressing;
I, gently daring
This sweetest confessing,
Say your garden at dusk
Is your soul, My Love."

VIRGINIA FOUNDATION FOR THE HUMANITIES AND PUBLIC POLICY

This project would not have been possible without a grant provided by the Virginia Foundation for the Humanities and Public Policy as part of its African-American Heritage Program. This program includes the African-American History in Virginia Grant Program, The African-American Heritage Database Project, and the African-American Heritage Trails Program, a partnership between VFH and the Virginia Tourism Corporation.

Through these programs, the Foundation seeks to increase understanding of African-American history in Virginia; to promote research and documentation of existing African-American historic sites; to strengthen the institutions that interpret African-American history in Virginia; and to encourage people from all parts of the nation and world to visit these sites.

For more information about the VFH and the African-American History Initiative and Heritage Trails project, write the Foundation's office at 145 Ednam Drive, Charlottesville, Virginia 22903, or call (434) 924-3296. Information about the VFH is also available on the internet at www.virginia.edu/vfh.

Virginia Foundation
for the Humanities and
Public Policy

ANNE SPENCER HOUSE AND GARDEN MUSEUM

The Anne Spencer home and garden at 1313 Pierce Street, Lynchburg, Virginia 24501, are open to the public. The garden is open daily at no cost. A brochure is provided at the garden for self-guided tours. Tours of the home are by appointment only. There is an admission fee. To make an appointment call (434) 845-1313.

The Anne Spencer House and Garden Museum, Inc., originally the Anne Spencer Memorial Foundation, became incorporated shortly after the house was designated a Virginia Historic Landmark in the fall of 1976. Its purpose is, in part, "to preserve and celebrate...the literary, cultural, and social legacy of Anne Spencer." Her son Chauncey continued to tell his mother's stories, and his own, from the house across the street where he lived until his death in 2002. Spencer's granddaughter, Carol Spencer Read, is active on the board of directors and regularly leads tours of the home. Other family members live nearby or in the region.

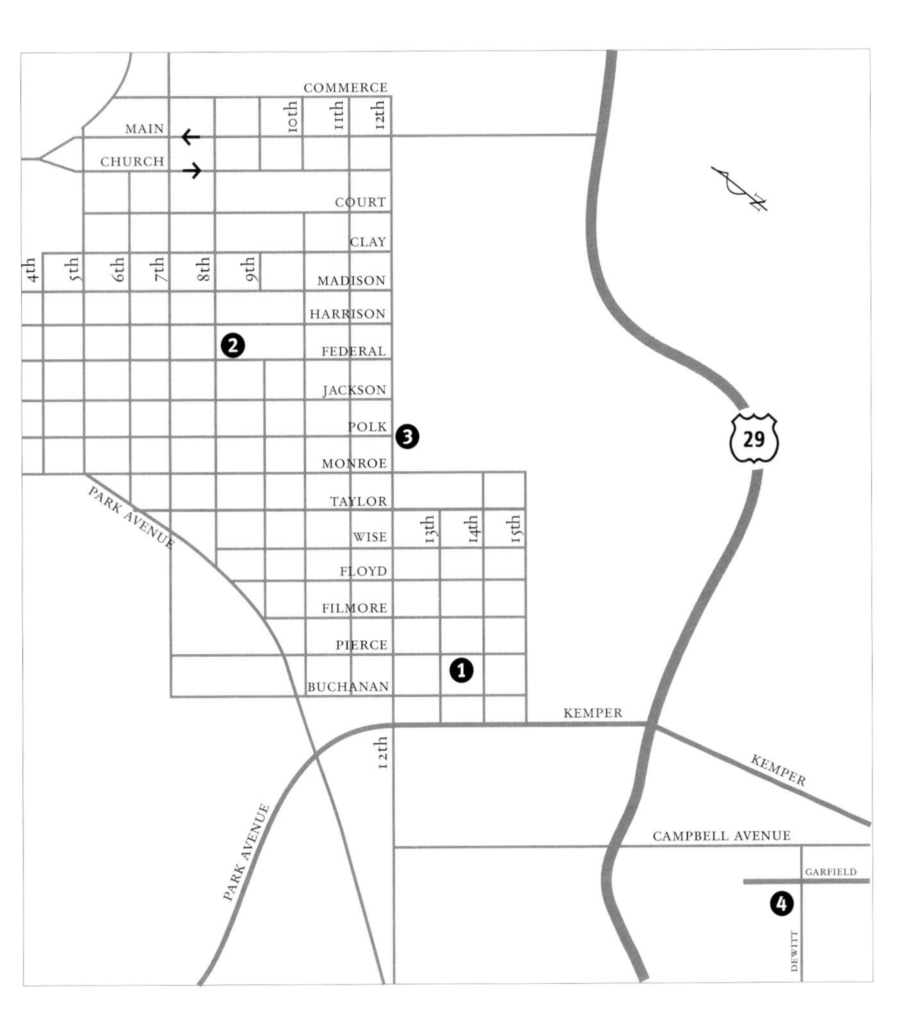

1. Anne Spencer House and Garden Museum at 1313 Pierce Street, between 12th and 13th Streets.
2. Eighth Street Baptist Church, Anne and Edward Spencer's church, at 801 Eighth Street, at the corner of Federal and 8th Streets.
3. Paul Laurence Dunbar Middle School For Innovation, the site of the former Dunbar High School where Anne Spencer served as librarian, at 1200-1208 Polk Street as it meets 12th Street.
4. Virginia University of Lynchburg, formerly Virginia Seminary, Anne Spencer's alma mater, at 2058 Garfield Avenue and Kelly Street.

CHAPTER ONE

1 As quoted in J. Lee Greene, *Time's Unfading Garden: Anne Spencer's Life and Poetry* (Baton Rouge and London: Louisiana State University Press, 1977), p. 10. Greene's biography of Anne Spencer is the definitive one. Our biographical account is heavily indebted to Greene's, which was based upon a wealth of primary source material, including many personal interviews with Anne Spencer.

2 The term "seminary," in the late 19th century, was used as a general designation for schools with a curriculum in humanities and science as well as theology. It did not necessarily refer to an institution solely for the education of clergy. For an informative history of Virginia Seminary, see Ralph Reavis, *Virginia Union University and Virginia University of Lynchburg: Two Paths to Freedom* (Richmond, Virginia: African American Publishers of Virginia, LLC, 2000.)

3 In a letter to an unknown correspondent dated March 2_, 1926, Anne Spencer remarked, "We have a lovely home – one that money ~~could~~ did not buy – it was born and evolved slowly out of our passionate, poverty-stricken agony to ~~have~~ own our own home and happiness."

4 Ted Delaney and Phillip Wayne Rhodes, *Free Blacks of Lynchburg, Virginia 1805-1865* (Lynchburg: Warwick House Publishing, 2001), pp. 30-31.

5 A succinct history of Lynchburg can be found in S. Allen Chambers, Jr., *Lynchburg, An Architectural History* (Charlottesville: University Press of Virginia, 1981). A useful popular history is Darrell Laurant, *A City Unto Itself, Lynchburg in the 20th Century* (Lynchburg: The News and Advance, 1997).

6 See Laurant, chap. 17.

7 The Crisis, XIX (Feb. 1920), p. 186.

8 Alain Locke, ed. *The New Negro* (New York: Atheneum Press, 1992), p. 148.

9 Richard Ellmann and Robert O'Clair, eds. *The Norton Anthology of Modern Poetry* (New York: W.W. Norton & Co., 1973), pp. 276-278.

10 Personal conversation with Prof. Carl Hester of the Religion Department of Randolph-Macon Woman's College, April 17, 2003.

11 While a number of unpublished poems have been lost, there remain a considerable number of fragments of poems, rough drafts, letters, and observations in the archives of the Anne Spencer House and Garden Museum, Inc. in Lynchburg, Virginia.

12 As quoted in Greene, p. 66.

13 Interview April 29, 2002, with Chauncey Spencer.

14 Greene, p. 159.

CHAPTER TWO

15 The following description of the 1930s garden is based upon Spencer family photographs from the 1920s through the 1950s and personal interviews with Anne Spencer's son, Chauncey Spencer, and his wife, Anne Spencer, on April 10 and 29 and June 12, 2002. Jane Baber White also shared photographs of the original garden housed in the Southern Memorial Association archives in Lynchburg and her research on the history of the garden, which informed its restoration in the early 1980s.

16 Anne Spencer's collection of garden magazines and nursery catalogs is located in the Spencer residence at 1313 Pierce Street. Several plans in *Garden and Home Builder*, XLII, 5 (Jan. 1926), 336-337, somewhat resemble Anne Spencer's garden in scale and spatial organization.

17 We are indebted to Professor K. Ian Grandison of the University of Virginia for calling these similarities to our attention. The standard work on the subject is Richard Westmacott, *African-American Gardens and Yards in the Rural South* (Knoxville: The University of Tennessee Press, 1992). Our comments on vernacular elements in the garden are also indebted to this work, especially chapters 3-6. Our information regarding Anne Spencer's gardening background is based on interviews with Anne Spencer's son and daughter-in-law, Chauncey and Anne Spencer, on April 10 and 29 and June 12, 2002.

¶ It is important to note that while there are some apparent similarities to African-American rural vernacular traditions in Anne Spencer's design; there are also major differences. For a more detailed perspective, the reader is referred to Richard Westmacott's study. Here it must suffice to draw a few contrasts. Rural vernacular African-American gardens are primarily utilitarian and contain mostly edible plants. Anne Spencer's garden in its 1930s and later version contained almost none and these were reserved for the birds. Rural vernacular gardens are mostly based on oral traditions and observation of gardens nearby. Anne Spencer consulted the popular garden design literature of her day, which she collected, and utilized technical information from nursery catalogs. Rural vernacular gardens have simple functional plans devoid of expensive ornamental plants, elegant architectural details, and subtle spatial arrangements. Obviously, in this respect they are far removed from Anne Spencer's sophisticated design. The setting and function of her garden are entirely different. Hers is an urban residential garden of an affluent family devoted to contemplation and hospitality, not a utilitarian garden to sustain a rural family.

18 A useful description of the Spencer house can be found in Chambers, *Lynchburg, An Architectural History*, pp. 406-408. Some details of our description are indebted to Chambers.

19 In the following description, the terms "cottage garden" and "pool garden" are convenient ways to identify some of the major garden "rooms." Anne Spencer herself did not use these terms to refer to these areas of her garden.

20 Nina V. Salmon, ed., *Anne Spencer: "Ah, how poets sing and die!"*, a collection of her poetry with commentary by Nina V. Salmon (Lynchburg: Warwick House Publishing, 2001), p. 66.

CHAPTER THREE

21 Interview June 12, 2002, with Anne Howard Spencer, wife of Chauncey Spencer and daughter-in-law of the poet, Anne Spencer, with whom she should not be confused.

22 Interviews April 29 and June 12, 2002, with Chauncey Spencer. All quotations from Chauncey Spencer in this chapter are from these interviews unless otherwise noted.

23 Johnson, p. 213.

24 *The Anne and Edward Spencer Story*, a video produced by Liberty Broadcasting Network, Inc., 1995.

25 Interview June 12, 2002, with Chauncey Spencer.

26 Interview June 12, 2002, with Anne Spencer, daughter-in-law.

27 Anne Spencer's close friend and fellow Harlem Renaissance poet, Mary Effie Lee, later Effie Lee Newsome, published in 1940 a volume of children's poetry titled *Gladiola Gardens*. Perhaps she was influenced by Anne Spencer to do so.

28 Salmon, p. 71.

29 Greene, p. 156.

CHAPTER FOUR

30 There are two major published collections of Anne Spencer's poetry. One is the appendix to J. Lee Greene's biography, *Time's Unfading Garden*. The other is Nina V. Salmon, ed., *Anne Spencer: "Ah, how poets sing and die!"*. We have cited Spencer's work in Salmon's collection, since it is more complete than Greene's.

31 Salmon, p. 36.

32 Greene, p. 162.

33 *The Lynchburg News*, Feb. 8, 1974, Section B, p. 3.

34 *The Crisis*, June 1922, as quoted in Cheryl A. Wall, *Women of the Harlem Renaissance* (Bloomington and Indianapolis: Indiana University Press, 1995), p. 56.
35 Brooks Atkinson, ed. *The Essential Writings of Ralph Waldo Emerson* (New York: Random House, Inc., Modern Library Paperback Edition, 2000), p. 6.
36 In a previously mentioned letter dated March 2_, 1926, Anne Spencer wrote, "I read garden and seed catalogs, Browning, Hausman, Whitman, *Saturday Evening Post*, detective tales, *Atlantic Monthly*, *American Mercury*, *Crisis* [sic], *Opportunity*, *Vanity Fair*, *Hibber's Journal*, oh, anything."
37 Greene, p. 113.
38 Countee Cullen, ed. *Caroling Dusk: An Anthology of Verse by Negro Poets* (New York: Harper and Brothers, 1927), p. 42.
39 "Lines to a Nasturtium" was inscribed on the wall of the Spencer's kitchen, the only one of her poems to be given such special treatment. A painting of a garland of nasturtiums surrounds the text of the poem.
40 Salmon, p. 37.
41 Salmon, p. 57.
42 Salmon, p. 41.
43 Salmon, p. 59.
44 Salmon, p. 70.
45 Genesis, chaps. 1-6. *The Holy Bible*, Revised Standard Version (New York: Thomas Nelson and Sons, 1959).
46 Salmon, p. 66.
47 Salmon, p. 50.
48 Salmon, p. 30. These lines are reminiscent of Keats's "Ode to a Nightingale." We are indebted to Marlon B. Ross, Professor of English and African-American Studies at the University of Virginia, for calling this similarity to our attention and for helping us clarify aspects of Anne Spencer's poetry by placing it in the context of nineteenth- and twentieth-century English and American poetry.
49 James Weldon Johnson, *The Book of American Negro Poetry* (New York: Harcourt, Brace and Company, 1931), p. 45.
50 Salmon, p. 32.
51 Salmon, p. 51.
52 Greene, pp. 67, 68.
53 Salmon, p. 35.
54 The Gospel according to Matthew, ch. 26, verse 38, *The Holy Bible*, Revised

Standard Version (New York, Thomas Nelson and Sons, 1946).

55 Other of Spencer's poems appear to imitate Dickinson's terse, compact expressions of a highly personal philosophy. We are indebted to Marlon B. Ross, Professor of English and African-American Studies at the University of Virginia for this observation.

56 Salmon, p. 52.

57 Salmon, p. 55.

58 In this poem we find distinct echoes of certain ideas and specific wording expressed in "Life-Long Poor Browning," "[Thou are come to us, O God, this year]," "Change," and "Substitution."

59 Jane Baber White called our attention to the manuscript, which is in the archives of the Southern Memorial Association.

60 Anne Spencer, "To John Keats, Poet, At Springtime," unpublished manuscript.

61 Interview on June 12, 2002, with Chauncey Spencer.

62 Greene, p. 65.

63 Johnson, p. 213.

64 Salmon, p. 40.

65 Salmon, p. 55.

CHAPTER FIVE

66 The following description of the garden's restoration is based upon Jane Baber White's article, "Restoration of a Poet's Garden," *American Horticulturist*, 66, 10 (Oct. 1987), 27-31, and several personal conversations with her in the summers of 2002 and 2003. We are also indebted to Jane White for providing numerous photographs from the Southern Memorial Association archives documenting the construction of the restored garden.

67 The poem is "Grapes: Still-Life," which can be found in Greene, p. 192, and Salmon, p. 57.

CHAPTER SIX

68 Cullen, p. 45.

69 Alexander Pope, "An Epistle to Lord Burlington" in John Dixon Hunt and Peter Willis, editors, *The Genius of the Place, The English Landscape Garden 1620-1820*, (Cambridge, Massachusetts and London: The M.I.T. Press, 1988), 211.

70 Chambers, 408.

71 Salmon, p. 39.

72 *The Anne Spencer Garden*, video narrated by Rebecca Frischkorn (Rubicon Productions, 2002).

CHAPTER SEVEN

73 Our dating of the poems and citing of their original place of publication is based on J. Lee Greene's *Time's Unfading Garden*, pp. 175-197.

74 "Lines to a Nasturtium," Anne Spencer's revision of the version first published in *Palms*, IV (October, 1926), 13.

75 "Grapes: Still-Life," first published in *The Crisis: A Record of the Darker Races*, XXXVI (April, 1929), 124.

76 "Creed," first published in Countee Cullen (ed.), *Caroling Dusk: An Anthology of Verse by Negro Poets* (New York: Harper, 1927), 51-52.

77 "Life-Long Poor Browning," first published in Countee Cullen (ed.), *Caroling Dusk: An Anthology of Verse by Negro Poets* (New York: Harper, 1927), 49-50.

78 "Questing," first published in Countee Cullen (ed.), *Caroling Dusk: An Anthology of Verse by Negro Poets* (New York: Harper, 1927), 48-49.

79 "Before the Feast at Shushan," first published in *The Crisis: A Record of the Darker Races*, XIX (February, 1920), 186.

80 "Requiem," first published in *Lyric* (Spring, 1931), 3.

81 "For Jim, Easter Eve," written in 1948 and first published in Langston Hughes and Arna Bontemps (eds.), *The Poetry of the Negro, 1746-1949* (Garden City, N.Y.: Doubleday, 1949), 65.

82 "Substitution," Anne Spencer's 1973 revision of the version first published in Countee Cullen (ed.), *Caroling Dusk: An Anthology of Verse by Negro Poets* (New York: Harper, 1927), 48.

COVER Anne Spencer House and Garden Museum, Inc., plan by Emmanuel Didier.

FRONTISPIECE Anne Spencer House and Garden Museum, Inc.

FIG. 1 Anne Spencer House and Garden Museum, Inc.

FIG. 2 Courtesy of Jane Baber White,
Archives of the Southern Memorial Association

FIG. 3 Private collection of Chauncey and Anne Spencer

FIG. 4 Courtesy of Jane Baber White,
Archives of the Southern Memorial Association

FIG. 5 Private collection of Chauncey and Anne Spencer

FIG. 6 Anne Spencer House and Garden Museum, Inc.

FIG. 7 Private collection of Chauncey and Anne Spencer

FIG. 8 Anne Spencer House and Garden Museum, Inc.

FIG. 9 Courtesy of Jane Baber White,
Archives of the Southern Memorial Association

FIG. 10 Courtesy of Jane Baber White,
Archives of the Southern Memorial Association

FIG. 11 Courtesy of Jane Baber White,
Archives of the Southern Memorial Association

FIG. 12 Courtesy of Jane Baber White,
Archives of the Southern Memorial Association

FIG. 13 Courtesy of Jane Baber White,
Archives of the Southern Memorial Association

FIG. 14 Courtesy of Jane Baber White,
Archives of the Southern Memorial Association

FIG. 15 Courtesy of Jane Baber White,
Archives of the Southern Memorial Association

FIG. 16 Courtesy of Jane Baber White,
Archives of the Southern Memorial Association

FIG. 17 Courtesy of Jane Baber White,
Archives of the Southern Memorial Association

FIG. 18 Courtesy of Jane Baber White,
Archives of the Southern Memorial Association

FIG. 19 Courtesy of Jane Baber White,
Archives of the Southern Memorial Association

FIG. 20 Courtesy of Jane Baber White,
Archives of the Southern Memorial Association
FIG. 21 Emmanuel Didier
FIG. 22 J. Lee Greene, frontispiece to *Time's Unfading Garden*
FIG. 23 Anne Spencer House and Garden Museum, Inc.
FIG. 24 Anne Spencer House and Garden Museum, Inc.
FIG. 25 Anne Spencer House and Garden Museum, Inc.
FIG. 26 Anne Spencer House and Garden Museum, Inc.
FIG. 27 Anne Spencer House and Garden Museum, Inc.
FIG. 28 Reuben M. Rainey
FIG. 29 Reuben M. Rainey
FIG. 30 Reuben M. Rainey
FIG. 31 Reuben M. Rainey
FIG. 32 Courtesy of Jane Baber White,
Archives of the Southern Memorial Association
FIG. 33 Reuben M. Rainey
FIG. 34 Reuben M. Rainey
FIG. 35 Reuben M. Rainey
FIG. 36 Reuben M. Rainey
FIG. 37 Reuben M. Rainey
FIG. 38 Reuben M. Rainey
FIG. 39 Reuben M. Rainey
FIG. 40 Reuben M. Rainey
FIG. 41 Reuben M. Rainey
FIG. 42 Reuben M. Rainey
FIG. 43 Reuben M. Rainey
FIG. 44 Courtesy of Jane Baber White,
Archives of the Southern Memorial Association
FIG. 45 Reuben M. Rainey
FIG. 46 Reuben M. Rainey
FIG. 47 Reuben M. Rainey
FIG. 48 Reuben M. Rainey
FIG. 49 Reuben M. Rainey
FIG. 50 Courtesy of Jane Baber White,
Archives of the Southern Memorial Association

FIG. 51 Courtesy of Jane Baber White,
Archives of the Southern Memorial Association

FIG. 52 Anne Spencer House and Garden Museum, Inc.

FIG. 53 Courtesy of Jane Baber White,
Archives of the Southern Memorial Association

FIG. 54 Courtesy of Jane Baber White,
Archives of the Southern Memorial Association

FIG. 55 Anne Spencer House and Garden Museum, Inc.

FIG. 56 Reuben M. Rainey

FIG. 57 Reuben M. Rainey

FIG. 58 Anne Spencer House and Garden Museum, Inc.

FIG. 59 Courtesy of Jane Baber White,
Archives of the Southern Memorial Association

FIG. 60 Rebecca T. Frischkorn

FIG. 61 Sandra Wilson

FIG. 62 Anne Spencer House and Garden Museum, Inc.

FIG. 63 Anne Spencer House and Garden Museum, Inc.

FIG. 64 Anne Spencer House and Garden Museum, Inc.

FIG. 65 Courtesy of Jane Baber White,
Archives of the Southern Memorial Association

FIG. 66 Courtesy of Jane Baber White,
Archives of the Southern Memorial Association

FIG. 67 Courtesy of Jane Baber White,
Archives of the Southern Memorial Association

FIG. 68 Courtesy of Jane Baber White,
Archives of the Southern Memorial Association

FIG. 69 Courtesy of Jane Baber White,
Archives of the Southern Memorial Association

FIG. 70 Courtesy of Jane Baber White,
Archives of the Southern Memorial Association

FIG. 71 Reuben M. Rainey

FIG. 72 Courtesy of Jane Baber White,
Archives of the Southern Memorial Association

FIG. 73 Reuben M. Rainey

FIG. 74 Courtesy of Jane Baber White,
Archives of the Southern Memorial Association

FIG. 75 Courtesy of Jane Baber White,
Archives of the Southern Memorial Association

FIG. 76 Reuben M. Rainey

FIG. 77 Anne Spencer House and Garden Museum, Inc.

FIG. 78 Courtesy of Jane Baber White,
Archives of the Southern Memorial Association

FIG. 79 Courtesy of Jane Baber White,
Archives of the Southern Memorial Association

BOOKS

Atkinson, Brooks, ed. *The Essential Writings of Ralph Waldo Emerson*. New York: Random House, Inc. Modern Library Paperback Edition, 2000.

Chamber, S. Allen, Jr. *Lynchburg, An Architectural History*. Charlottesville: University Press of Virginia, 1981.

Cullen, Countee, ed. *Caroling Dusk: An Anthology of Verse by Negro Poets*. New York: Harper and Brothers, 1927.

Delaney, Ted and Phillip Wayne Rhodes. *Free Blacks of Lynchburg, Virginia 1805-1865*. Lynchburg: Warwick House Publishing, 2001.

Greene, J. Lee. *Time's Unfading Garden: Anne Spencer's Life and Poetry*. Baton Rouge: Louisiana State University Press, 1977.

Huggins, Nathan Irvin. *Harlem Renaissance*. New York: Oxford University Press, 1973.

Hughes, Langston and Arna Bontemps, eds. *The Poetry of the Negro, 1746-1949*. Garden City, N.Y.: Doubleday and Co., 1949.

Hunt, John Dixon and Peter Willis, eds. *The Genius of the Place, The English Landscape Garden 1620-1820*. Cambridge, Massachusetts and London: The M.I.T. Press, 1988.

Johnson, James Weldon. *Along This Way, The Autobiography of James Weldon Johnson*. New York: Da Capo Press, 1973.

Johnson, James Weldon. *The Book of American Negro Poetry*. New York: Harcourt, Brace and Company, 1931.

Laurant, Darrell. *A City Unto Itself, Lynchburg in the 20th Century*. Lynchburg: The News and Advance, 1997.

Locke, Alain, ed. *The New Negro*. New York: Atheneum, 1992.

Newsome, Mary Effie Lee. *Gladiola Gardens: Poems of Outdoors and Indoors for Second Grade Readers*. Illustrated by Lois Maillou Jones. Washington, D.C.: Associated Publishers, 1940.

Reavis, Ralph. *Virginia Union University and Virginia University of Lynchburg: Two Paths to Freedom*. Richmond, Virginia: African American Publishers of Virginia, LLC, 2000.

Salmon, Nina V., ed. *Anne Spencer: "Ah, how poets sing and die!"* Lynchburg: Warwick House Publishing, 2001.

Tripp, Steven Elliott. *Yankee Town, Southern City, Race and Class Relations in Civil War Lynchburg*. New York and London: New York University Press, 1997.

Wall, Cheryl A. *Women of the Harlem Renaissance*. Bloomington and Indianapolis: Indiana University Press, 1995.

Westmacott, Richard. *African-American Gardens and Yards in the Rural South*. Knoxville: The University of Tennessee Press, 1992.

MAGAZINE ARTICLES

Briggs, Loutrel W. “Fitting the Prize Offer House with a Garden,” *Garden and Home Builder*, XLII, 5 (Jan. 1926).

Forsell, Mary. “Stanzas from a Southern Garden,” *Victoria*, X, 4 (April 1996), 74-79.

Greene, J. Lee. “Anne Spencer of Lynchburg,” *Virginia Cavalcade*, Spring 1978, 178-185.

McCormick, Kathleen, “Spencer’s Gifts,” *Historic Preservation*, 46, 1, (Jan./Feb., 1994), 66-69, 92-94.

Roades, Antoinette, “Beyond the Garden Gate,” *Rural Living, Prince George Electric Cooperative*, Feb. 1997, 12-14, 33.

Shields, Hatsy, “Women of Action,” *House Beautiful*, 141, 10 (Oct. 1999), 58-60, 170-171.

VIDEOCASSETTES

The Anne and Edward Spencer Story, produced by Liberty Broadcasting Network, Inc. 1995, 1 hr., 21-1/2 min., VHS videocassette.

The Anne Spencer Garden, produced by Rubicon Productions, narrated by Rebecca Frischkorn, 2002, 14 min., VHS videocassette.

Echoes from the Garden, The Anne Spencer Story, edited by Barnard K. Bangley, written by J. Lee Greene, Ph. D., narrated by Brenda Wilson, project directed by L. Garnell Stamps, 28-1/2 min., VHS videocassette.

THE AUTHORS

Rebecca T. Frischkorn has practiced landscape design for 26 years and currently resides in Charlottesville, Virginia. She frequently lectures to various civic organizations and is currently producing a series of programs for public television on the cultural significance of American gardens.

Reuben M. Rainey has taught history of landscape architecture at the University of Virginia for 25 years. His publications cover a wide range of topics including Italian Renaissance gardens, 20th century American landscape architecture and historic preservation.